NUCLEAR NONPROLIFERATION

A PRIMER

Gary T. Gardner

Lynne Rienner Publishers • Boulder & London

Published in the United States of America in 1994 by
Lynne Rienner Publishers, Inc.
1800 30th Street, Boulder, Colorado 80301

and in the United Kingdom by
Lynne Rienner Publishers, Inc.
3 Henrietta Street, Covent Garden, London WC2E 8LU

Library of Congress Cataloging-in-Publication Data
Gardner, Gary T., 1958–
    Nuclear nonproliferation : a primer / by Gary T. Gardner.
    Includes bibliographical references and index.
    ISBN 1-55587-478-9 (alk. paper)
    ISBN 1-55587-489-4 (pbk. : alk. paper)
    1. Nuclear nonproliferation. I. Title.
JX1974.73.G374   1994
327.1'74—dc20   93-23571
                                                             CIP

British Cataloguing in Publication Data
A Cataloguing in Publication record for this book
is available from the British Library.

Printed and bound in the United States of America

   ∞   The paper used in this publication meets the requirements
       of the American National Standard for Permanence of
       Paper for Printed Library Materials Z39.48-1984.   5 4 3 2

For Mom, Dad, Jeff, and Clarence,
my family

Contents

Tables and Figures

TABLES

FIGURES

Preface

The effort to control the spread of nuclear weapons has been more successful in the past half century than many dared hope, and is more firmly institutionalized today than ever before. Still, new challenges, stemming from changes in technology, governments, and international politics, appear constantly on the horizon. Common to all these challenges is the problem of providing access to nuclear technology for peaceful purposes while preventing its diversion to military use.

The changing face of nonproliferation created by international events such as the Gulf War and the breakup of the Soviet Union creates a demand for new blood in the field, including both area and topical specialists, and requires educational resources geared to these newcomers. This primer forms part of that educational effort. An initiative of the CIS Nonproliferation Project of the Monterey Institute of International Studies, this book was originally intended as an introduction to the field for the project's core group of aspiring nonproliferation specialists in the former Soviet Union. The effort has grown, however, into a broad-based introduction useful to a much larger audience: students, journalists, and others new to the field can profit from the information presented here. This primer presumes no previous experience with nuclear issues but presupposes an interest in serious study of the field. It provides a comprehensive overview of nonproliferation, from the technical basics to the history and politics of nonproliferation efforts.

Because the science of nuclear energy is at the heart of the nonproliferation challenge, the primer begins with a simple introduction to nuclear fission in Chapter 1, followed by descriptions of the nuclear fuel cycle and nuclear reactors in Chapters 2 and 3. Readers averse to scientific topics may begin their study later in the book, but are likely to return eventually to the technical sections as the need to comprehend the fundamentals of nuclear power becomes evident.

Following the technical sections, the book shifts to a look at historical and political issues. Chapter 4 describes the history of efforts to control the spread of nuclear materials and technology, and Chapter 5 examines the major legal structures emanating from that history. Chapter 6 deals with international nuclear safeguards, a critical confidence-building element of the nonproliferation regime. The politics of nonproliferation, including strategies for dealing with proliferation, is treated in Chapter 7.

The last three chapters deal with the most current issues in the regime. Chapter 8 discusses the critical 1995 Non-Proliferation Treaty (NPT) extension conference, at which the fate of the NPT will be determined. Chapter 9 describes the attitudes toward nonproliferation and nuclear capabilities of selected nations of proliferation concern. Chapter 10 closes with a brief description of current challenges to the nonproliferation regime. A summary chapter, an appendix containing the text of the NPT, an annotated bibliography, and a glossary provide ready reference information.

It is our hope that this effort will stimulate readers to pursue further study of the nonproliferation of nuclear weapons. Questions or comments are welcome and should be addressed to:

Program for Nonproliferation Studies
Monterey Institute of International Studies
425 Van Buren Street
Monterey, CA 93940.

This educational effort was made possible by grants from the Carnegie Corporation, the Compton Foundation, the John Merck Fund, the Ploughshares Fund, the W. Alton Jones Foundation, and the Winston Foundation. The views expressed herein, however, are those of the author and are not necessarily shared by these institutions.

* * *

The nonproliferation community is a supportive and generous one. Many individuals in that community were helpful in reviewing portions of the manuscript. I am particularly indebted to George Bunn, David Fischer, Chris Fitz, Lynn Huizenga, Betsy Perabo, William Potter, Leonard Spector, Roland Timerbaev, Frank Von Hippel, and Carl Walters for their comments and suggestions. Roger Haney provided expert computer graphics advice. None is in any way responsible for the final product, but all deserve acknowledgment and a rich note of thanks.

Special gratitude is in order for three of the individuals mentioned above. William Potter granted me a large block of undisturbed time to work on the project when he might have preferred that my energies were directed elsewhere. For his confidence and support, I am thankful. David Fischer was tremendously generous in his review of several chapters and offered highly detailed and invaluable comments on them. His assistance went far beyond what I could rightly expect. Finally, Betsy Perabo walked with me through the entire process and was unfailing in her encouragement of the effort. Her good cheer, consistent support, and timely humor made the project a lot of fun. I am indeed lucky to have such a good friend.

Gary T. Gardner

1

Nuclear Fission and the Nuclear Bomb

Nuclear proliferation is a problem of global proportions, but initial approaches to the subject can be made on a much smaller scale—the scale of the atom. Nuclear physics reveals the enticing and problematic power of this fundamental building block of matter. This chapter introduces the basics of nuclear energy and discusses their relationship to the issue of nuclear proliferation.

FISSION AS A SOURCE OF ENERGY

The crucial event in harnessing nuclear energy, whether in a nuclear reactor or a nuclear bomb, is the splitting of an atom. This action, known as nuclear fission, releases tremendous energy—millions of times more than that of a chemical reaction.[1] In fact, the fissioning of atoms in one pound of uranium releases as much energy as the burning of 6,000 barrels of oil or 1,000 tons of coal.[2] The enormous power of the atom makes nuclear energy a tempting resource for energy ministries and military establishments worldwide.[3]

Splitting the atom, however, is no simple task. Many difficulties inherent in the fission process must be overcome by any nation or group intending to harness the power of the atom, whether for military or peaceful purposes. A simple description of these difficulties follows a brief review of the structure of an atom.

THE STRUCTURE OF AN ATOM

Most atoms consist of protons, neutrons, and electrons. Protons and neutrons bond together strongly to form a nucleus, and electrons orbit around them. The number of protons gives an atom, or element, its unique identity and family name. All uranium atoms, for example, have 92 protons, and any atom with 92 protons must be a uranium atom. If a proton is added to an atom or taken from it, the atom's identity changes completely.

Neutrons, on the other hand, can vary in quantity in the same kind of atom. Some uranium atoms, for example, have 143 neutrons, some 146. If protons establish an element's distinctive identity—its surname—neutrons give a twist to that identity, like a first name.

Atoms of the same family are called isotopes. For example, the uranium isotope U-235 is made up of 92 protons and 143 neutrons, whereas the more common U-238 has 92 protons and 146 neutrons. (The designations "235" and "238" are obtained by adding together the numbers of protons and neutrons in the nucleus.) Both U-235 and U-238 belong to the uranium family, but each has certain distinctive attributes.

U-235 is highly unstable, which makes it easier to split than its sister isotope U-238. In a reactor, a neutron fired at a U-235 atom attaches itself to the atom, increasing its instability, which in turn causes the atom to break apart (fission) and release energy. The same neutron directed at the more stable U-238 atom would likely be absorbed without fissioning. Many neutrons are intercepted benignly by U-238 atoms, and others are absorbed by the atoms of other materials in the reactor. Still others escape from the reactor completely (see Figure 1.1). In sum, the fission process might be imagined as involving the following components:

- the "targets": U-235 atoms, whose capture and fissioning releases the atomic energy
- the "arrows": neutrons, which attack the U-235 targets or seek to escape
- the "interceptors": U-238 atoms, which defend the U-235 targets by absorbing neutron "arrows"[4]

The fissioning of a U-235 atom in turn releases two or three of its own neutrons. If at least one of these is successful in splitting another U-235 atom, a chain reaction is established, which produces a steady output of energy in a nuclear reactor (see Figure 1.2). If the chain reaction involves enough atoms in a fraction of a second, as in a nuclear bomb, a tremendous explosion results. Because of its easy fissibility, U-235 is generally more valuable than U-238 to those interested in generating nuclear energy.

OBSTACLES TO FISSION

The unstable U-235 atom, however, is quite rare, constituting only a tiny fraction of the atoms in a chunk of natural uranium. In fact, the "interceptor" isotope U-238 is 140 times more common in natural uranium than the

Figure 1.1 Three Possible Destinies of a Neutron in a Reactor Environment

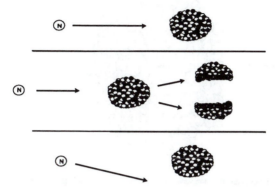

Neutrons are absorbed by a U-238 atom (top), by a U-235 atom (middle), or by reactor material (bottom). In the middle case, neutron absorption causes the U-235 to become unstable and split.

Figure 1.2 A Nuclear Chain Reaction

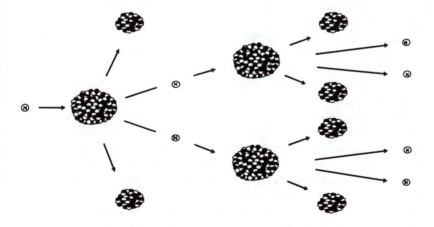

Each fissioned atom releases neutrons, some of which go on to split other atoms.

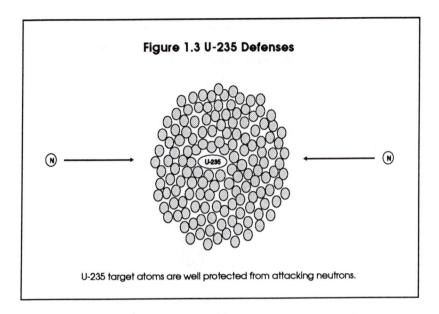

Figure 1.3 U-235 Defenses

U-235 target atoms are well protected from attacking neutrons.

fissile "target" U-235. The rare U-235 atoms in natural uranium, then, are well defended against incoming neutrons by the abundant U-238 atoms (see Figure 1.3). In addition, the attacking neutrons are ill suited for their mission: most fly far too fast to attach themselves to a U-235 atom.

Without human intervention, the situation is not at all favorable for sustained fissioning of the U-235 atom: on the one hand, formidable defenses in the form of U-238 atoms and other neutron-absorbing materials keep most neutrons away from the target U-235, and on the other, the attacking neutrons are largely incapable of penetrating and splitting an atom, even if they can reach it. Any hope of harnessing the tremendous power of the atom requires the creation of more favorable conditions for a sustainable nuclear chain reaction.

Several adjustments are possible. One is to slow the attacking neutrons to a speed where interacting with U-235 becomes possible. (Slow neutrons can more easily attach themselves to an atom than fast neutrons can.) In a nuclear reactor, this is done with the moderator, a material such as light water, heavy water, or graphite, which surrounds the nuclear fuel in the reactor core.[5] When neutrons collide with the heavy water or graphite atoms, the neutrons decelerate to a speed that greatly improves their chances of attaching to a U-235 atom and causing it to break apart. In reactors moderated by these materials, no other adjustments are necessary to make fission possible.

When light (ordinary) water is used as a moderator, however, some neutrons are slowed, but others are absorbed by the neutron-hungry light-water atoms. Thus a reactor moderated by light water is still a neutron-hostile environment, as the neutron faces probable absorption either by U-238 or light-water atoms. However, because ordinary water is plentiful and cheap compared to heavy water, which is costly and very difficult to make, light water is the preferred moderating material. To make use of light water, however, a second strategy must be employed to increase the chance of a successful fission.

This second strategy is to set up more targets, that is, to increase the proportion of U-235 found in uranium. The greater the share of U-235 atoms in uranium fuel or bomb material, the more likely a successful chain reaction can be started. A process called enrichment is used to raise the proportion of U-235 from its natural level of 0.7 percent to around 3–5 percent for use in a light-water reactor, or to around 90 percent for use in a nuclear bomb. With enriched uranium fuel, enough U-235 is available for fissioning even after neutron losses to light-water atoms are taken into account.

Finally, in a variant on the enrichment option, the fission process may be assisted by increasing the proportion of U-235 targets so much that even fast neutrons cannot miss them. If the percentage of U-235 is increased to 90 percent or higher, neutrons are able to fission the U-235 without being slowed by a moderator. The use of fast neutrons and highly enriched uranium (along with plutonium, discussed shortly) is characteristic of nuclear bombs and of the so-called fast reactor.

NEUTRONS AND PLUTONIUM PRODUCTION

Another important event in the reactor core that increases the chances of successful fission is the transforming action of attacking neutrons. We have seen that neutrons that are unsuccessful in splitting U-235 atoms are absorbed by U-238 atoms or other materials, or they escape the reactor entirely. The neutrons captured by U-238 are not entirely wasted, however. Having failed to find and split a U-235 nucleus, these neutrons serve a secondary purpose: to convert the nonfissile U-238 into fissile plutonium (Pu-239), a process requiring two steps, which take a few days. Once this transmutation is achieved, another fissile target has been created for other flying neutrons to attack. In fact, approximately 30 percent of the power generated by a nuclear reactor comes from the fissioning of plutonium created through this transmutation process. The same process takes place when thorium, which is occasionally used in nuclear fuel, absorbs a neutron and eventually creates U-233, another fissile element.

In short, nature supplies only one fissile isotope—U-235—but scientists have created two others, Pu-239 and U-233. All three are useful, in varying degrees, for generating nuclear power, and all three can contribute to a nuclear explosive capability.

THE PROLIFERATION SIGNIFICANCE
OF NUCLEAR MATERIALS

The preceding discussion of obstacles to successful fission identifies several strategies for assisting the fission process. Four materials used in these strategies are usually safeguarded because of their possible contribution to building a nuclear weapon:

- *Plutonium.* One of the most proliferation-significant materials in the nuclear fuel cycle, plutonium can be used directly in a nuclear bomb. "Weapons-grade" plutonium, with a high percentage of Pu-239, is relatively easy to handle and produces the highest explosive yield per unit of material. "Reactor-grade" plutonium, with levels of Pu-239 lower than that found in weapons-grade material, can be used to build a relatively low-yield (but still quite deadly) nuclear explosive.
- *Highly enriched uranium.* Uranium enriched to 20 percent or more U-235 is considered highly enriched. Enrichment to 93 percent U-235 is normally required for use in a bomb. However, even 20 percent U-235 is considered sensitive because relatively little extra work is required for further enrichment to the dangerous 93 percent U-235 level.
- *Low-enriched uranium.* Although low-enriched uranium cannot be used in a nuclear weapon, it is only one step (further enrichment) away from possible use as weapons material.
- *Heavy water.* Although not used in nuclear weapons, heavy water allows natural uranium to be burned in a nuclear reactor, and makes the production of plutonium possible without an expensive and technologically complex uranium enrichment plant. Thus heavy water can be thought of as a substitute for a uranium enrichment plant.[6]

  Heavy water is also sensitive because it produces tritium when used as a moderator. Tritium can be used as a "booster" for nuclear explosives: it boosts the explosive yield of a given quantity of fissile material. Tritium can also be used to reduce the amount of plutonium or enriched uranium needed to make a nuclear weapon.

THE BASICS OF AN ATOMIC BOMB

Although nuclear reactors and atomic bombs both rely on the same fission process for release of energy, their management of the fission is distinctly different. Nuclear reactors are designed to shut themselves off before they exceed their structural capability. Atomic bombs, on the other hand, are designed to keep the fission process going until their materials are so hot that they vaporize, reach a very high pressure, and then explode.[7] The uncontrolled fissioning process in a nuclear bomb is possible only when a certain amount of fissile material, called a critical mass, is present. At subcritical amounts of fissile material, many neutrons escape and leave too few neutrons available to fission other atomic nuclei. A critical mass of nuclear material, however, is large enough to maintain a nuclear reaction even after neutrons are lost to the outside environment.[8]

The amount of fissile material needed for an atomic bomb depends on several factors. First, different types of fissile material (U-235, U-233, or Pu-239) have different critical masses. The critical mass of Pu-239, for example, is only one-fifth that of U-235; therefore, much less plutonium than uranium is needed to construct a bomb. Second, compressed fissile material has a lower critical mass than material at normal density. Thus bombmakers can stretch limited fissile resources by compressing them to critical mass levels. Third, reflectors can be used in the bomb to deflect escaping neutrons back into the mass of material and involve them in the fission process. And finally, tritium can be used in the weapon as a sort of "neutron supplement" to provide additional neutrons to accelerate the chain reaction. The critical mass for the three fissile materials under various conditions is shown in Table 1.1.

Table 1.1   Critical Mass for U-235, U-233, and Pu-239 Under Various Conditions (in kilograms)

	U-235	U-233	Pu-239
Normal density, unreflected	52	16	10
Compressed to double density	13	4	2.5
Using reflectors	13–25	5–10	5–10

Sources: Nuclear Weapons Databook, Volume 1: U.S. Nuclear Forces and Capabilities (Cambridge, Mass.: Ballinger Publishing Co., 1984), p. 24; F. Von Hippel, personal correspondence, July 25, 1992, p. 1.

The plutonium route to development of a nuclear weapon has been taken by the United Kingdom, France, India, and probably Israel, whereas South Africa, Brazil, Argentina, Iraq, and Pakistan have all pursued (and in the last case is still pursuing) the enriched uranium route to a bomb.

Fission bombs are of two types. The gun-barrel design uses conventional explosives to propel a subcritical mass of uranium down a barrel for collision with another subcritical mass. The bomb dropped on Hiroshima was of this type.[9] (Table 1.2 compares the nuclear yields of various bomb types with that of the Hiroshima bomb.)

The other fission bomb design is an implosion device, in which conventional explosives and reflectors surround a subcritical mass of nuclear material. When the explosives are detonated simultaneously, the pressure on the central core of nuclear material is so great that it compresses the material to criticality.[10] Under appropriate conditions, the rate at which fissions occur then increases greatly and energy is released so rapidly that a nuclear explosion results.

Table 1.2 Comparative Nuclear Yields

	Yield	Relation to Hiroshima bomb
Hiroshima bomb	12–15 Kt	—
Limit imposed by TTB Treaty	150 Kt	11.1 times larger
First hydrogen bomb test	10.4 Mt	770 times larger
Largest nuclear test (USSR)	58 Mt	4296 times larger
Smallest U.S. nuclear weapon	0.25 Kt	54 times smaller

Source: Compiled from *Nuclear Weapons Databook, Volume 1: U.S. Nuclear Forces and Capabilities* (Cambridge, Mass.: Ballinger Publishing Co., 1984), pp. 32–34.
  Notes: Kt = kiloton, mt = megaton, TTB = Threshold Test Ban. Last column is calculated using 13.5 Kt as the estimated size of the Hiroshima bomb.

SUMMARY

From the perspective of atomic physics, nuclear proliferation is simply the spread of particular materials and technologies that facilitate the fission of atomic nuclei. Any element or technology that increases the number of fissile U-235 atoms in nuclear fuel, creates Pu-239 or U-233, or improves the chances of free-flying neutrons hitting a fissile atom is of concern. The difficulties in managing these materials and technologies are especially great because most can be used for both military and peaceful purposes. Because atomic physics provides no means to distinguish fission for peaceful purposes from fission for military ends, solutions to this dilemma have been sought in the political and legal realm; these are discussed in later chapters of this book.

NOTES

1. Anthony Nero, *A Guidebook to Nuclear Reactors* (Berkeley: University of California Press, 1979), p. 4.
2. Ibid.
3. Even more energy is released if very light atoms can be fused together. This process—nuclear fusion—is the basis for thermonuclear explosives (the hydrogen

bomb), which are many times more powerful than fission bombs. Although fusion, or hydrogen, bombs are an integral part of the arsenals of the major nuclear weapon states, the economic and industrial resources necessary and the level of technological complexity involved make them impractical and unobtainable in almost every other case. In fact, development of a fission reaction is necessary in order to "trigger" fusion. Because civilian uses of fusion energy are still only a distant prospect, and fusion-based weapons can only follow the development of fission, this book will focus on the nonproliferation threat from nuclear fission.

4. One important characteristic of the neutron does not fit the analogy: the neutron does not split an atom by force in the way an arrow would split an apple. In fact, a slow neutron is more likely than a fast one to fission an atom. This is because the slow neutron is able to attach itself to the atom and make it unstable enough to break apart. The fast neutron is likely to be deflected from the target atom.

5. Heavy water is made up, in part, of hydrogen atoms that contain one neutron, whereas the hydrogen in light (ordinary) water has no neutrons. This gives each different moderating properties.

6. However, another technologically complex facility—a plutonium reprocessing plant—is necessary to extract plutonium from spent fuel for use in a nuclear bomb. Thus, heavy water is of much greater proliferation concern when coupled with a reprocessing capability than when it is not. Chapter 3, Nuclear Reactors, considers this question further.

7. C. Walter, personal correspondence, July 15, 1992.

8. Cochran, Arkin, and Hoenig, *Nuclear Weapons Databook, Volume 1*, p. 24.

9. Ibid., p.26.

10. Ibid.

2

The Nuclear Fuel Cycle

The diversion of nuclear material from peaceful to military use is more likely at some types of nuclear facilities than at others. This chapter gives an overview of the life cycle of nuclear fuel, from its origin as natural uranium to its final state as nuclear waste, and assesses the proliferation risks associated with each stage.

THE ONCE-THROUGH VERSUS PLUTONIUM FUEL CYCLES

A simplified version of the fuel cycle, with modifications for different reactor types, is shown in Figure 2.1. In the basic cycle, uranium is mined, refined, processed into an appropriate chemical form, converted into fuel rods, fissioned (burned) in a reactor, and stored as waste. However, variations on this cycle are necessary to accommodate different reactor types, and these variations introduce proliferation concerns. The uranium enrichment stage, for example, is needed to prepare fuel for use in light-water reactors, whereas heavy-water production is needed to supply the moderator for heavy-water reactors. In addition, both reactor types may operate on a once-through fuel cycle, in which spent reactor fuel is not recycled, or on a plutonium fuel cycle, which provides for extraction and reuse of plutonium from spent fuel rods. This extraction process is an additional sensitive stage in the fuel cycle known as reprocessing.

The plutonium fuel cycle is controversial. Its proponents argue that it requires far less fresh uranium fuel and produces lower quantities of nuclear waste than a once-through fuel cycle. Opponents claim that waste levels under the two systems are similar. More significantly, opponents worry that the vast quantities of recycled plutonium made available at power plants all over the world would significantly increase the chances of diversion to illicit purposes. They point out that all fissile material in the once-through fuel cycle remains in a form not directly usable for nuclear weapons.[1]

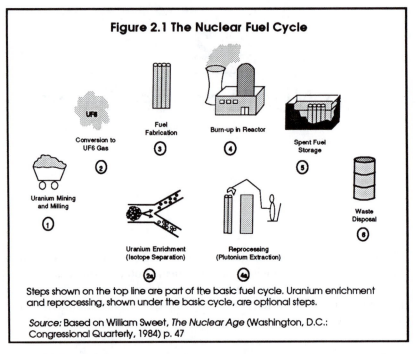

Figure 2.1 The Nuclear Fuel Cycle

Steps shown on the top line are part of the basic fuel cycle. Uranium enrichment and reprocessing, shown under the basic cycle, are optional steps.

Source: Based on William Sweet, *The Nuclear Age* (Washington, D.C.: Congressional Quarterly, 1984) p. 47

In the United States, opponents of the plutonium fuel cycle carried the day in the 1970s, proscribing commercial plutonium reprocessing for both domestic use and export and severely curtailing U.S. development of the breeder reactor, which is designed to generate reusable plutonium fuel. Since then, development of the breeder reactor elsewhere in the world has slowed for economic reasons. Today, only a handful of nations possess reprocessing plants, and fewer still plan to base their nuclear power programs on the recycling of nuclear fuel.

THE FUEL CYCLE
FROM A NONPROLIFERATION PERSPECTIVE

The fuel cycle stages illustrated in Figure 2.1 are described below. Heavy-water production, which is not strictly a part of the fuel cycle, is addressed last.

• Mining and Milling

Uranium ore is found in the earth's crust and must be mined like any other mineral. Excavated ore is milled to separate uranium from foreign matter; the uranium is then processed into a chemical form (U_3O_8) called yellowcake, named for its amber color.

Facility locations. The world leaders in uranium mining and milling are Canada, the United States, Australia, France, Niger, Namibia, and South Africa.[2] Virtually all countries contain minable uranium deposits, although extraction of the uranium ore may not be cost effective.

Nuclear material's vulnerability to theft (by persons unconnected with the facility). About 5,000 kilograms (kg) of natural uranium are needed to produce the 25 kg of weapons-grade uranium required for one atomic bomb.[3] Diversion of this quantity of natural uranium without detection by facility authorities would be highly difficult.

Nuclear material's vulnerability to diversion (by persons connected with the facility). Diversion by facility authorities would not be difficult, particularly because most uranium mines and processing centers are not subject to international safeguards.

Proliferation risk. Very low. In isolation, this stage poses virtually no proliferation risk because natural uranium cannot be used to make an atomic weapon.

• Conversion

At the conversion stage, the processed natural uranium is converted to a form usable in a nuclear reactor. If the material is intended for use in a heavy-water reactor, which burns natural (nonenriched) uranium, it is converted to uranium metal or uranium dioxide (UO_2). Uranium destined for light-water reactors is converted to uranium hexafluoride, a gas suitable for enrichment.

Facility locations. The nations with the highest uranium conversion capacity are Canada, France, the United States, and the United Kingdom.[4] A complete list of such nations is given in Table 2.1

Nuclear material's vulnerability to theft. Same as for mining and milling.

Nuclear material's vulnerability to diversion. At an unsafeguarded facility, material could be diverted easily to military purposes. At a safeguarded facility, diversion would likely be detected.

Proliferation risk. Very low. Because the percentage of U-235 in the converted uranium is still extremely low, the material cannot be used directly in the production of nuclear weapons. However, International Atomic Energy Agency (IAEA) safeguards take effect at this stage.

Table 2.1 Global Nuclear Fuel Cycle Capacities

Country	U Ore Processing (tU/y)	U Refining and Conversion (tU/y)	U Enrichment (swu/y)	Fuel Fabrication (tHM/y)	Reprocessing (tHM/y)	Heavy-water Production (t/y)
Argentina	220/125	55/150	20/100	300	0/5	0/450
Australia	5,745	ul	ul	ul	ul	ul
Belgium	50	ul	ul	435	0/100	ul
Brazil	840	90	0/10	100	ul	ul
Canada	17,100	31,200	ul	3,250/250	ul	106/356
China	1,100	ul	200	ul	ul	ul
France	5,640/550	28,350	10,800	1,775/120	1,600/1,600	ul
Gabon	1,100	ul	ul	ul	ul	ul
Germany	0/125	ul	580	1,445	0/40	ul
India	200	50	ul	410	275/1,000	314/295
Italy	ul	ul	ul	460	10	ul
Japan	0/60	206	252	1,549/35	0/800	ul
Mexico	0/200	ul	ul	2	ul	ul
Morocco	470/370	ul	ul	ul	ul	ul
Namibia	4,000	ul	ul	ul	ul	ul
Netherlands	ul	ul	1,200	ul	ul	ul
Niger	4,600	ul	ul	ul	ul	ul

(continued)

Table 2.1 cont.

Country	U Ore Processing (tU/y)	U Refining Conversion (tU/y)	U Enrichment (swu/y)	Fuel Fabrication (tHM/y)	Reprocessing (tHM/y)	Heavy-water Production (t/y)
Norway	ul	ul	ul	ul	ul	**4**
Pakistan	**30**	ul	**5**	ul	ul	ul
Portugal	**170**	ul	ul	ul	ul	ul
South Africa	**3,148**/3,200	**700**	**300**	ul	ul	ul
South Korea	ul	**200**	ul	**200**	ul	ul
Spain	**190**	ul	ul	**200**	ul	ul
Sweden	ul	ul	ul	**400**	ul	ul
Turkey	ul	**1**	ul	ul	ul	ul
UK	ul	**2,200**/5,500	**850**	**1,830**/6	**1,508**/850	ul
USA	**11,415**/18,760	**25,190**	**19,200**/770	**3,750**/360	**5,100**/1,800	**190**
USSR	ul	ul	**10,000**	**700**	ul	ul
Yugoslavia	**120**	ul	ul	ul	ul	ul

Source: Nuclear Engineering International, *World Nuclear Industry Handbook, 1992* (New York: Reed Business Publishing, 1992), pp. 127–128. Figures accurate as of August 31, 1991.

Note: Bold figures indicate operable capacity. Unbolded figures indicate capacity under construction or shut down. Planned capacity is not shown. ul (unlisted) indicates that no figure was given in the original source, either because the information was unavailable, or more often, because no capacity was in operation, under construction, or shut down for the nation in question. t = 1,000 kg. HM = heavy metal. SWU = separative work units.

• Enrichment

The enrichment stage is particularly sensitive: it is the first moment at which uranium takes on the fissile properties needed for use in a nuclear bomb. Enrichment is a process designed to raise the share of the desired fissile U-235 in uranium from its natural level of 0.7 percent to the much higher levels needed for use in a nuclear reactor or a nuclear bomb. (These levels range from 1.8 percent for use in some Russian-built reactors to 3 percent for most light-water reactors to more than 90 percent for use in a nuclear bomb.)

Although weapons-grade uranium has thirty times more U-235 than light-water reactor-grade uranium, it is not thirty times more difficult to manufacture. Once an enrichment capacity is in place, it can be modified to produce highly enriched uranium, although this is more difficult for some types of enrichment technology than for others.[5] (See the elaboration on the enrichment process that follows this overview.)

Facilities locations. Principal nations involved in uranium enrichment are the United States, France, Russia, the Netherlands, and the United Kingdom. Nations of proliferation concern that possess an enrichment capacity include Argentina, Brazil, and Pakistan. See Table 2.1 for a complete listing of such nations.

Nuclear material's vulnerability to theft. As noted in the previous chapter, an atomic explosive requires as little as 13 kg of uranium enriched to more than 90 percent U-235, a mass of material easily handled by one person. Security at enrichment plants, however, is extremely tight.

Nuclear material's vulnerability to diversion. Material from unsafeguarded enrichment plants can be diverted easily to military purposes. Material under IAEA safeguards can also be easily diverted to proscribed uses, but not without a high likelihood of detection.

Proliferation risk. High. Enrichment facilities have the potential to produce weapons-grade uranium. (However, even highly enriched uranium hexafluoride cannot be used directly in an atomic bomb. It must first be converted to uranium oxide or uranium metal.[6]) The high proliferation potential of the enrichment stage has led Nuclear Suppliers Group (NSG) member-states to place an unofficial embargo on the export of enrichment technology.

• Fuel Fabrication

Before enriched uranium or plutonium can be used in a nuclear reactor, it must be fabricated into fuel rods. The enriched uranium, plutonium, or natural uranium (used in heavy-water reactors) is shaped into cylindrical pellets, which are then stacked in tubes called fuel rods. The rods are then bundled together into fuel assemblies.

Facilities locations. The leading nuclear fuel fabrication plants are located in the United States, Canada, France, the United Kingdom, Japan, and Germany. Nations of proliferation concern that have fabrication plants include Argentina, Brazil, and India. See Table 2.1 for a complete listing of such nations.

Nuclear material's vulnerability to theft. Light-water reactor fuel assemblies each weigh from 440 to 1,100 pounds. They are shipped on open trailer trucks, with each pair of assemblies enclosed in steel containers to prevent damage. The total weight of two assemblies and their container is about three tons.[7] Diversion of fuel assemblies would require heavy-duty transport and handling equipment.

Nuclear material's vulnerability to diversion. Unsafeguarded fuel assemblies could easily be diverted to military uses. The diversion of safeguarded assemblies would likely be detected, but not prevented, by international safeguards.

Proliferation risk. Low to high. Fuel rods fabricated for use in heavy-water reactors contain natural (nonenriched) uranium, whereas those destined for use in light-water reactors contain low-enriched uranium. Neither type of uranium can be directly diverted to a nuclear weapon. Fuel rods fabricated for use in a breeder reactor contain various isotopes of plutonium, but with sufficient Pu-239 and Pu-241 content to be of high proliferation concern.[8]

• Fuel Burn-up

Once in the reactor core, the fuel rods are irradiated as a controlled fission reaction process is begun. Approximately 180 fuel assemblies containing about 110 tons of uranium are needed to fuel a typical 1,000 megawatt (MW) light-water reactor for three years.[9] The quantity of fissile uranium is reduced as the fuel is burned up, but plutonium is produced in its place.

Facility locations. At the end of August 1991, 431 power reactors were in operation and 71 were under construction around the world.[10]

Nuclear material's vulnerability to theft. Fissile material is probably less vulnerable to theft during reactor operation than at any other point in the fuel cycle because the fuel assemblies are inaccessible (in all but the Canadian heavy-water reactor) and radioactive period.[11] Most reactors must be shut down to remove the fuel rods; this cannot be done without attracting attention.

Nuclear material's vulnerability to diversion. In an unsafeguarded reactor, material easily could be diverted to military uses. In a safeguarded reactor, diversion would likely be detected.

Proliferation risk. Low to high. In isolation, a nuclear reactor using natural or low-enriched uranium is not a proliferation danger; it contains no nuclear material that could be diverted directly to production of a nuclear explosive. In combination with a reprocessing capability, however, the fuel in a nuclear reactor is of proliferation concern. Reactors using highly enriched uranium are of great concern.

• Spent-fuel Storage

After burn-up, the fuel rods must be replaced with fresh fuel. Depleted of U-235 but rich in plutonium, the rods are removed from the reactor and cooled for several months in pools of fresh water. Although this storage is intended to be temporary, no permanent waste disposal site has been chosen anywhere in the world.

Facility locations. Temporary spent-fuel storage ponds are generally located on the grounds of the nuclear reactor from which the spent fuel was taken. So-called "away from reactor" spent-fuel storage sites are found in the United Kingdom, France, Sweden, Germany, Finland, the United States, the former Czechoslovakia, and Japan.[12]

Nuclear material's vulnerability to theft. Although laden with plutonium, spent fuel rods are not attractive targets for thieves. The rods are highly radioactive and unwieldy. Moreover, spent fuel is of use in the manufacture of nuclear explosives only if there is a reprocessing plant, and most nations with reprocessing plants have their own supply of spent fuel.

Nuclear material's vulnerability to diversion. From an unsafeguarded spent-fuel storage plant, material could be diverted to military uses (assuming access to a reprocessing facility) with no problem. In a safeguarded facility, diversion would likely be detected.

Proliferation risk. Medium. In isolation, a spent-fuel storage facility is not a great proliferation risk. Only in combination with a reprocessing capability is spent fuel of proliferation concern.

• Reprocessing

Spent-fuel rods are removed from storage pools and sent to a reprocessing plant for plutonium extraction. The rods are cut into pieces and dissolved in acid.[13] Using the Plutonium Uranium Recovery by Extraction (PUREX) method, more than 90 percent of the uranium and plutonium in the spent-fuel solution can be recovered.[14] Uranium emerging from this process typically contains only 1 percent U-235, far below the level needed for a nuclear bomb, and even too weak for use in a light-water reactor. The plutonium exiting a reprocessing plant, however, can be converted to a form usable for nuclear weapons.

Facility locations. Russia, France, and the United Kingdom are the world leaders in reprocessing. Japan has a strong interest in reprocessing and is currently constructing a large reprocessing plant at Rokkasho-Mura. India has several small reprocessing plants, and Argentina is constructing one. See Table 2.1 for a complete list of nations with reprocessing capabilities.

Nuclear material's vulnerability to theft. Reprocessing of the highly radioactive spent fuel is done by remote control from behind thick walls; the separated plutonium and uranium are virtually inaccessible during this operation.[15] Following reprocessing, the materials enter a more accessible packaging area where 10-liter cylinders about one meter long are filled with 2.5 kg of plutonium solution. Each cylinder weighs 14 kg when filled. Their stainless steel shipping containers, however, weigh about 180 kg.[16]

Nuclear material's vulnerability to diversion. Unsafeguarded material in a reprocessing plant could easily be diverted to a nuclear weapons program. Diversion of safeguarded material would likely be detected.

Proliferation risk. High. Plutonium extracted from low burn-up fuel (e.g., from a production reactor or a heavy-water, natural-uranium research reactor) is directly usable in a nuclear weapon. Plutonium derived from the high burn-up fuel of the standard light-water reactor is not the preferred material for nuclear weapons, but it could be used as a nuclear explosive by a party not concerned with obtaining the highest possible efficiency or yield.[17] (See also Chapter 3, Nuclear Reactors.) Plutonium reprocessing technology is another highly sensitive technology; its export is unofficially embargoed by the Nuclear Suppliers Group.

• Waste Disposal

After the uranium and plutonium are removed, the fuel rod residue, which contains more than forty radioactive isotopes, must be safely disposed of.

Because a permanent waste disposal solution has not been found for this high-level waste (HLW), most of it is "temporarily" stored in pools at the facilities that produced it. Permanent waste disposal sites in outer space, in the sea bed, or underground have been proposed.

Facility locations. Currently, a permanent nuclear waste disposal facility is being considered in Nevada for U.S. waste, and another facility is planned in Germany. Permanent waste disposal facilities for low-level waste (LLW, including rags, gloves, filters, and similar materials that have been exposed to radiation but do not require special shielding) and intermediate-level waste (ILW, including solidified sludges, equipment, and metal fragments whose level of radioactivity is lower than that of HLW, but still require special shielding) are operating in France, Sweden, Germany, and the United States.[18]

Nuclear material's vulnerability to theft. HLW's vulnerability to theft is likely to be similar to that of spent fuel. If the waste has been reprocessed, however, it is a much less attractive target for theft because the plutonium has been removed from it.

Nuclear material's vulnerability to diversion. Same as for spent fuel.

Proliferation risk. Low. The high level of radioactivity coupled with the depleted state of uranium and plutonium left in the waste make diversion of the material for the construction of a nuclear bomb unattractive.

• *Heavy-water Production*

Although technically not a part of a fuel cycle, heavy-water production deserves mention as an important auxiliary component of the heavy-water reactor fuel cycle. Because reactors moderated by heavy water can fission natural uranium, the expensive and difficult step of enriching uranium is unnecessary. Heavy-water production is itself a difficult process, but is not beyond the capability of most industrialized nations.

Facility locations. India is the world leader in heavy-water production capacity, although its plants are plagued by frequent breakdowns.[19] The United States, Canada, Russia, and Norway also produce heavy water. Argentina has a long-delayed plant under construction. (See Table 2.1 for a listing of heavy-water production capacities.)

Heavy water's vulnerability to theft. Several hundred cubic meters of heavy water are used to moderate a medium-sized heavy-water reactor.[20] Presumably, theft of such a massive quantity of material is more likely in transit, when the mode of transport itself could be commandeered, than at the reactor site.

Heavy water's vulnerability to diversion. Unsafeguarded heavy water could easily be diverted. Diversion of safeguarded heavy water presumably would be detected, although several instances of long-hidden heavy-water diversions to third parties have been revealed. A German trader, for example, is known to have bought Soviet-origin heavy water in quantities of less than one ton—the level that triggers IAEA safeguards. The material was then shipped to India.

Proliferation risk. High. Heavy water, like a uranium enrichment plant, can serve as a critical link in the chain of processes needed to convert natural uranium into plutonium, and the tritium extracted from heavy water can be used to reduce the amount of fissile material needed to create a nuclear explosive.

A CLOSER LOOK AT ENRICHMENT TECHNOLOGIES

Uranium can be enriched in several ways. Common to all methods is the effort to separate some of the nonfissile U-238 atoms from the rest of the uranium stock, so that what remains has a higher percentage of the desirable U-235 atoms. The four most commonly used uranium enrichment methods are gaseous diffusion, gas centrifuge, aerodynamic, and laser.

• Gaseous Diffusion

The most widely used enrichment method, gaseous diffusion dates back to the Manhattan Project. Uranium in a gaseous form called uranium hexafluoride is forced through a series of membranes, each of which allows the lighter U-235 atoms to pass through more easily than the heavier U-238 atoms. After penetrating each membrane, the gas is richer in U-235 than it was originally, but only slightly: 1,250 passes are needed to enrich the gas to 3 percent U-235, the enrichment level used in most light-water nuclear power plants, whereas 4,000 passes are required to enrich the material to the weapons grade of 90 percent U-235.[21]

Proliferation significance. Gaseous diffusion is a technically complex process that requires massive amounts of electricity. (The two U.S. enrichment facilities still in operation each use about 5,000 MW of electricity, as much as is consumed by a city of several million people.[22]) These barriers make clandestine acquisition of a gaseous diffusion plant difficult.[23] In addition, it is difficult, although not impossible, to modify a gaseous diffusion plant that produces low-enriched uranium to produce highly enriched uranium.[24] Still, as with all enrichment facilities, gaseous diffusion plants are of proliferation concern because of their capacity to produce weapons-grade uranium.

• Gas Centrifuge

The gas centrifuge uses centrifugal force to draw U-238 atoms away from the desired U-235. When uranium gas is spun in a centrifuge, the heavier U-238 atoms gravitate toward the outer walls, whereas the lighter U-235 atoms remain in the center. The centrifuge method requires only 35 repetitions to achieve weapons-grade uranium, and a plant with 1,000 centrifuges can supply the uranium stock for several nuclear weapons per year.[25] On the downside, the technology requires a high level of technical precision, and it is difficult to maintain.

Proliferation significance. The relatively low power requirements of the gas centrifuge method of enrichment, coupled with its relative efficiency, make it an enrichment process of high proliferation concern.

• Aerodynamic Methods

Like the gas centrifuge enrichment method, aerodynamic methods use centrifugal force to separate some U-238 from the bulk of the uranium stock. Uranium gas is blown over a curved surface, which has the effect of separating the heavier U-238 from the lighter U-235. Six hundred repetitions of this process are needed to achieve 3 percent U-235 enrichment, and 2,000 stages are needed for 90 percent enrichment. Although aerodynamic methods such as the Becker nozzle and Helikon are less technologically complex than gaseous diffusion or the gas centrifuge, they require the most energy of all the processes under consideration.[26]

Proliferation significance. Because of the tremendous energy requirements of aerodynamic methods and their relatively inefficient operation, other methods of enrichment are likely to be preferred.[27]

• Laser

Still in the development stages, the laser method of enrichment uses different light waves to excite particular atoms while leaving others unaffected. The excited atoms can then be separated from the others. This method is so precise that only one pass is necessary to complete the enrichment process, and it can be used on "tailings," or wastes remaining from other plants.[28]

Proliferation significance. Laser enrichment technology appears to be out of the reach of most nations of current proliferation concern. However, its high efficiency and relatively low energy requirements could make it the enrichment method of choice as it becomes more widely available.

NOTES

1. Anthony Nero, *A Guidebook to Nuclear Reactors* (Berkeley: University of California Press, 1979), p. 191.

2. Nuclear Engineering International, *World Nuclear Industry Handbook, 1992,* p. 127.

3. F. Von Hippel, personal correspondence, July 25, 1992, p. 2.

4. Nuclear Engineering International, *World Nuclear Industry Handbook, 1992,* p. 127.

5. William C. Potter, *Nuclear Power and Nonproliferation: An Interdisciplinary Perspective* (Cambridge, Mass.: Oelgeschlager, Gunn & Hain, Publishers, 1982), p. 81.

6. Mason Willrich and Theodore B. Taylor, *Nuclear Theft: Risks and Safeguards* (Cambridge, Mass.: Ballinger Publishing Co., 1974), p. 18.

7. Ibid., p. 34.

8. C. Walter, personal correspondence, July 15, 1992.

9. Willrich and Taylor, p. 34.

10. Nuclear Engineering International, p. 11.

11. Willrich and Taylor, p. 35.

12. Nuclear Engineering International, p. 128.

13. Willrich and Taylor, p. 35.

14. Potter, p. 78.

15. Willrich and Taylor, p. 35.

16. Ibid., p. 36.

17. D. Fischer, personal correspondence, July 15, 1992, p. 3.

18. International Atomic Energy Agency, "Radioactive Waste Management" (Vienna: IAEA Division of Public Information), p. 3.

19. D. Fischer, personal correspondence, July 15, 1992, p. 3.

20. This figure is based on data from a sample of CANDU (Canadian deuterium uranium) reactors listed in Nuclear Engineering International, *World Nuclear Industry Handbook,* pp. 91, 93, and 104.

21. Potter, pp. 71–72.

22. F. Von Hippel, personal correspondence, July 25, 1992, p. 3.

23. Potter, p. 72.

24. Ibid., p. 81.

25. Ibid., p. 72.

26. Ibid., pp. 72–73.

27. Ibid., p. 73.

28. Ibid., pp. 73–74.

3

Nuclear Reactors

Although reactors are not the most proliferation-prone facilities in the nuclear fuel cycle, the assorted reactor types worldwide do present a variety of proliferation concerns. Following a brief description of the operation of a nuclear reactor and a review of reactor functions, this chapter discusses the proliferation significance of various reactors in operation today.

REACTOR OPERATION AND PURPOSES

Nuclear reactors are made in many types and sizes, but the basic elements and processes involved are similar in most models (see Figure 3.1). *Fuel* in the form of uranium, plutonium, or a mixture of these is placed in the reactor core, where neutrons from these materials are used to split, or fission, the fuel's atoms. A *moderator,* usually water or graphite, surrounds the fuel and slows down (moderates) neutrons in the fuel to increase the chances of a successful fission. *Control rods* filled with neutron-absorbing substances such as boron are inserted into the core to regulate the fission process and to shut down the reactor if necessary. Finally, a *coolant,* which is sometimes the same material as the moderator, is flushed through the hot fuel rods of power reactors to carry away heat. In a power reactor the coolant is run through a heat exchanger, which generates steam to spin a *turbine*. The turbine generates electricity.

Nuclear reactors are commonly associated with electricity production, but they have a variety of other uses as well. The first clue to the proliferation significance of a nuclear reactor is found by examining the declared purpose of the unit.

Power reactors. Most reactors are used to produce electricity through the process described above. No single characteristic of a power reactor makes it a proliferation concern; its proliferation danger depends on the

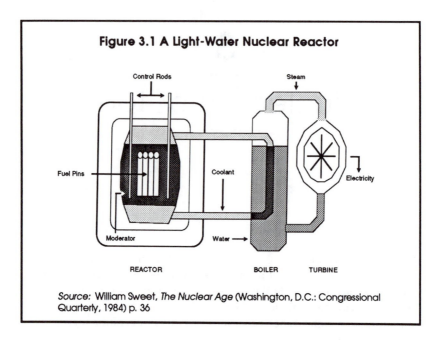

Figure 3.1 A Light-Water Nuclear Reactor

Control Rods

Steam

Fuel Pins

Coolant

Electricity

Moderator

Water →

REACTOR   BOILER   TURBINE

Source: William Sweet, *The Nuclear Age* (Washington, D.C.: Congressional Quarterly, 1984) p. 36

type of fuel and moderator used, the amount of plutonium produced, and the refueling process used for the reactor.

Plutonium production reactors. All reactors whose fuel contains U-238 produce weapons-usable plutonium as a by-product. A plutonium production reactor, however, is designed to produce material ideally suited for use in weapons.[1] Thus a plutonium production reactor is obviously of high proliferation concern. The United Kingdom once used the plutonium production reactor for power production; however, it is inefficient and uneconomical for this purpose.

Research reactors. Research reactors are used for training purposes or for the production of radioactive isotopes with medical or biological applications. Research reactors are typically 1–5 MW—a size that yields low quantities of plutonium-laden spent fuel. Despite these apparently innocuous characteristics, some research reactors encompass the most dangerous proliferation characteristics of all: a heavy water–moderated, natural uranium–fueled, low fuel burn-up research reactor is of particular concern (see below). Coupled with a reprocessing capability, a research reactor can be a dangerous, proliferant technology.

Materials test reactors. Because materials used in a reactor core undergo great stress from constant neutron bombardment, new materials are regularly tested to determine their suitability for use in a nuclear reactor.

These materials are best tested in a reactor environment, and a materials test reactor is designed for this purpose. The spent fuel from a materials test reactor yields small amounts of plutonium, which could be used in a nuclear bomb.

Submarine reactors. Nuclear submarines are propelled by small light-water reactors, the kind of reactor used to generate electric power. Unlike most light-water power reactors, however, submarine reactors are fueled by highly enriched uranium (HEU), which can be used in a nuclear weapon. For this reason they are of great proliferation significance.

It should be stressed that in isolation most reactors present no proliferation problem unless they are fueled with plutonium or highly enriched uranium.[2] If the nuclear fuel entering the reactor is not weapons-usable, and if a nation has no capacity to extract plutonium from spent fuel, the reactor itself can do little to advance a nuclear weapons capability. Still, in combination with other facilities, reactors can become an integral part of a nuclear weapons program. See Chapter 2, The Nuclear Fuel Cycle, for a description of these other facilities.

A PROLIFERATION ANALYSIS OF NUCLEAR REACTORS

The declared purpose of a nuclear reactor gives a preliminary idea of its proliferation significance, but other reactor characteristics reveal more about the reactor's potential for use in a nuclear bomb program. The five questions discussed below help to clarify further the proliferation potential of a nuclear reactor.

• *What Kind of Fuel Does the Reactor Use?*

First, a reactor's proliferation significance can be assessed by looking at the type of fuel it uses. Some of the nuclear fuels described below were discussed in Chapter 1.

Natural uranium. Natural uranium is not usable in a nuclear weapon, and poses no direct proliferation threat. (Historically, however, most reactor-generated weapons material has come from reactors fueled by natural uranium, especially the heavy-water reactor, described below.[3])

Low-enriched uranium. Low-enriched uranium cannot be used in a nuclear weapon. It is no more dangerous for proliferation than natural uranium, unless the state is also operating an enrichment plant. In that case low-enriched uranium can be converted into feedstock for the enrichment plant. This would permit the production of highly enriched uranium (weapons-grade material) more quickly, in larger quantities, and with much less energy than if natural uranium were used as the feedstock.[4]

Highly enriched uranium or plutonium.   Both highly enriched (greater than 93 percent) uranium and plutonium are weapons-usable materials. Reactors using either material as fuel are of greater proliferation concern than other reactors because potential weapons material is present both before and after fuel burn-up.

• What Kind of Moderator Does the Reactor Use?

Identification of the material used to moderate a nuclear reaction is helpful in assessing a reactor's proliferation significance. Recall that sustained fission of uranium occurs when neutrons fly slowly enough to split the nucleus of a U-235 atom, and that the atoms of the moderating material slow the speedy neutrons by colliding with them. Thus the moderator is a "support" material, which helps make fission possible. Three materials are commonly used as moderators: light water, heavy water, and graphite.

Light water.   Light (ordinary) water poses no proliferation threat.

Heavy water.   Heavy water poses two proliferation problems. First, it is transformed into tritium when bombarded with neutrons in a nuclear reactor. Tritium can be used to boost the explosive power of nuclear weapons, in effect reducing the amount of fissile material needed to make a nuclear explosive. The second concern is more indirect and applies only when a heavy-water reactor is used in conjunction with a reprocessing capability. A reactor moderated by heavy water can be fueled by natural uranium, thereby eliminating the need for a uranium enrichment plant. Thus a nation with access to a reprocessing capability might view a heavy-water power plant as a relatively direct way to convert natural uranium to plutonium.

Graphite.   Reactor-grade graphite presents the same indirect proliferation problem as heavy water: it allows the use of natural uranium fuel and therefore allows a nation to omit the difficult step of uranium enrichment.

• How Much Fissile Material Does the Reactor Consume and How Much Does It Produce?

The ratio of material produced to material consumed in a reactor is important from a nonproliferation perspective. In regard to this conversion ratio, there are basically three categories of nuclear power plants: burners, converters, and breeders.[5] Burners and converters are also commonly categorized as "thermal" reactors. Breeders are "fast" reactors, a reference to the fast (un-moderated) neutrons used to fission atoms in a breeder reactor's core.

Burners. Reactors that consume more fissile material than they produce in their spent fuel are called burners. Light-water reactors, for example, produce approximately six units of plutonium for every ten units of U-235 consumed by the reactor. The conversion ratio of burners is of relatively low proliferation concern because burners consume more potential bomb material than they produce.

Converters. Converters are reactors that yield about the same amount of fissile material as they consume.

Breeders. Breeders are net producers of fissile material; that is, they yield more plutonium than they consume. Breeders represent a substantial proliferation threat: not only do they create more fissile material than they use, they also use highly enriched uranium or plutonium as fuel. In other words, weapons-usable material is present at a breeder reactor site before and after fuel burn-up, from fuel loading to spent-fuel storage. Breeders are not widely used today, although at one time they were viewed as a promising solution to energy shortages because of their virtually inex-haustible yield of fuel for nuclear reactors.

• Must the Reactor Be Shut Down for Refueling?

Reactor refueling is a critical operation from a proliferation perspective because sensitive fissile materials, particularly plutonium, are vulnerable to diversion as they are moved in and out of the reactor. Two refueling procedures are of particular interest: off-line and on-line.

Off-line refueling. In most reactors, core fissile material is accessible only when the reactor is shut down (off-line), which makes secret diver-sion of the material difficult.[6] These reactors typically require a four- to six-week shutdown for refueling. Reactor shutdown, in effect, warns ob-servers to watch for possible diversion of fissile material.

On-line refueling. Reactors that can be refueled without being shut down can facilitate clandestine diversion of fissile material from the reac-tor core because the core material is accessible at all times.

• How Long Is Fuel Burned in the Reactor?

The duration of fuel burn-up provides important information about the quality of plutonium extracted from a reactor and its suitability for use in a bomb. The longer reactor fuel is burned, the more it becomes contaminated with nonfissile Pu-238, Pu-240, and Pu-242. At the same time, the share of the desirable, fissile isotope Pu-239 decreases (see Table 3.1). Plutonium with a long fuel burn-up is known as "reactor-grade" plutonium. Plutonium produced after a short fuel burn-up and containing a high percentage of Pu-239 is known as "weapons-grade" plutonium.

Table 3.1 Share of Isotopes in Weapons- and Reactor-Grade Plutonium

Isotope	Weapons-grade (low burn-up) plutonium	Reactor-grade (high burn-up) plutonium	Generally fissile?
Pu-238	—	2	no
Pu-239	94	58	yes
Pu-240	6	27	no
Pu-241	—	8	yes
Pu-242	—	5	no

Source: C. Walter, personal correspondence, July 15, 1992, p. 3.

The suitability of high burn-up plutonium for use in a bomb is still debated. The United States demonstrated in the 1960s that contaminated, reactor-grade plutonium could be used in a nuclear bomb, but the level of contamination in the tested plutonium was not revealed.

What is certain is that reactors that burn fuel for short periods are of greater proliferation concern than those that burn fuel for extended intervals. Most reactors can be run for short or long periods, but the declared purpose of the reactor gives some idea of how long a unit normally remains on-line.

Power reactors. Reactors dedicated to power production remain on-line for as long as possible in order to minimize refueling costs and non–revenue-producing off-line time. Their plutonium tends to be relatively highly contaminated, and is the least attractive for use in a bomb.

Production reactors. At the opposite extreme are production reactors, which are run for short periods in order to produce weapons-grade plutonium. Production reactors are worrisome because of their declared purpose of weapons material production; on the other hand, they would not be used by a nation seeking a clandestine route to the bomb.

Research reactors. The most worrisome technology for clandestine production of weapons-grade plutonium is the research reactor. Experiments run with research reactors often require frequent reactor shutdown.

During these shutdown times, fuel rods could be extracted after only a short burn-up. Thus a research reactor is ideally suited to the clandestine production of weapons-grade plutonium (assuming the state has access to a reprocessing capability). Oversized research reactors are of particular concern.

A TAXONOMY OF NUCLEAR REACTORS

Armed with a framework for analyzing the proliferation threat posed by nuclear reactors, we turn to the proliferation significance of specific reactor types. Consideration of several of the questions presented above may be necessary for a full understanding of the proliferation dangers of each reactor type. Table 3.2 presents a summary of the proliferation-sensitive characteristics of the four reactor types.

Table 3.2 Proliferation-Sensitive Characteristics of Four Reactor Types

	Fuel	Moderator	Refueling
Light-water reactors—LWR (PWR and BWR), VVER	*Low-enriched uranium* (enriched to about 3% U-235)	Light (natural) water	Requires plant shutdown
Heavy-water reactors—CANDU, etc.	Natural (nonenriched) uranium	*Heavy water* (deuterium oxide)	*No plant shutdown required*
Gas-cooled reactors	Natural to *slightly enriched uranium*	*Graphite*	Requires plant shutdown
Fast breeder reactors	*Plutonium* or *highly enriched uranium*	None	Requires plant shutdown

Note: Italics indicate a material or process subject to IAEA safeguards or otherwise of proliferation concern.

• Light-water Reactors

By far the most common power reactor in use today, the light-water reactor (LWR) accounts for 77 percent of power reactors worldwide.[7] LWRs are commonly divided into two types: the pressurized-water reactor (PWR), accounting for about 52 percent of reactors worldwide, and the boiling-water reactor (BWR), representing about 25 percent of the world market.[8] The difference between the two is inconsequential from a proliferation standpoint.

Westinghouse was an early leader in the development of the PWR, in part because its PWR design was selected over General Electric's BWR for use in the U.S. Navy's first nuclear submarines. Westinghouse later licensed Framatome of France, Siemens/KWU of West Germany, and other

European firms to develop its technology in Europe. Today these firms are world leaders in their own right in the development of light-water technology. Other U.S. firms involved in light-water reactor design include Babcock and Wilcox and Combustion Engineering. The Russian version of the light-water reactor is known as the VVER.

The light-water reactor

- uses low-enriched uranium as fuel
- uses light, or ordinary, water as the moderator
- is typically a burner reactor, consuming more fissile material than it produces (conversion ratio is 0.6)[9]
- must be shut down for refueling
- replaces one-third of its fuel every year (three-year burn-up cycle)[10]

On all counts the LWR is one of the more proliferation-resistant reactors, and no nation is known to have used it to manufacture material for a nuclear weapon.[11] None of the fissile material entering or leaving the plant is directly usable in a nuclear weapon, although the spent fuel could be reprocessed to remove weapons-usable plutonium. The LWR burns more fissile material than it produces—another attractive feature—and it must be shut down for refueling, which alerts observers to the potential for fissile material diversion. In addition, for economy's sake fuel is left in an LWR as long as possible, making it highly radioactive and increasing the level of contaminating isotopes (Pu-240 and Pu-242) in the spent fuel. Thus a long-burning PWR produces reactor-grade, rather than weapons-grade, spent fuel. (Recall, however, that reactor-grade plutonium can also be used in a nuclear explosive; it is simply less efficient.) In sum, in isolation, or with international safeguards covering an LWR's fissile material, this reactor poses a very low proliferation threat.

• Heavy-water Reactors

Heavy-water power reactors account for about 6 percent of the power reactors worldwide, and are found primarily in Canada. India, Argentina, Pakistan, and South Korea have units as well, and Romania has five plants under construction. Historical and geological factors have combined to make Canada the world leader in heavy-water reactor technology. During World War II, Canadian scientists working on the Manhattan Project specialized in research in heavy-water applications.[12] This expertise, combined with Canada's rich deposits of uranium, made nuclear power a viable energy alternative for Canada without the need to invest in the complex and expensive process of uranium enrichment. Today, the CANDU (Canadian deuterium uranium) reactor model is the world's leading heavy-water power reactor.

The heavy-water reactor

- uses natural uranium fuel
- uses deuterium oxide (heavy water) as the moderator
- is typically a burner reactor, consuming more fissile material than it produces (conversion ratio is 0.75–0.80)[13]
- can be refueled without shutdown
- has a 15-month burn-up cycle[14]

In isolation, the heavy-water reactor is a relatively proliferation-resistant reactor. No enriched uranium is involved, and its on-line refueling feature is not likely to be a problem without a reprocessing plant to extract plutonium from spent fuel. In combination with a reprocessing capability, however, the HWR becomes a more worrisome technology—more so, in fact, than most reactor types discussed here.

Consider the position of a nation with a heavy-water reactor and a reprocessing plant: (1) Heavy-water reactors produce twice the amount of plutonium per year of operation as an LWR of equivalent size.[15] (2) The spent fuel containing this plutonium is more easily divertible from an HWR reactor, especially a research reactor, than is the case in an LWR. (3) If burned for a short time, as in a research reactor, the plutonium extracted from spent fuel would be weapons-grade, meaning it will perform more predictably in a nuclear weapon than the reactor-grade plutonium taken from reactors that burn for a longer period.[16] (4) Tritium can be harvested from the reactor's irradiated heavy water and used to reduce the quantity of fissile material needed for a nuclear explosive.

These characteristics, in addition to the HWR's simplicity of design and operation, make it a proliferation-problematic reactor when a reprocessing capability is assumed. In fact, reactors fueled by natural uranium and moderated by heavy water or graphite (see below, gas-cooled reactors) have been used more than any other reactor type to produce nuclear weapons material.[17] Israel, India, Taiwan, South Korea, and North Korea have all tried at one time or another to produce weapons-grade plutonium using heavy-water reactors.

• Gas-Cooled Reactors

Whereas the LWR was the reactor of choice in the United States in the 1950s, France and the United Kingdom pursued development of the gas-cooled reactor, a potentially more efficient unit that did not require expensive enriched uranium fuel, available at that time only from the United States.[18] France abandoned the effort in favor of light-water reactors, but the United Kingdom stayed the course, although recently it has also begun to turn to light-water reactors.

The gas-cooled, graphite-moderated reactor

- uses natural uranium fuel
- is moderated by graphite
- is typically a burner, consuming more fissile material than it produces (conversion ratio is 0.7)[19]
- is typically shut down for refueling
- replaces one-fourth of its fuel every year (a four-year burn-up cycle)[20]

The proliferation danger inherent in a gas-cooled reactor is similar to that in the heavy-water reactor. The gas-cooled reactor is of simple design, and produces easily processed spent fuel. In fact, early model reactors of this type were used to produce weapons-grade plutonium. Furthermore, the gas-cooled reactor requires neither heavy water nor enriched uranium. It is therefore an attractive technology for a nation seeking to reduce dependence on foreign supplies of nuclear materials or technology. North Korea is said to have copied gas-cooled reactor technology for this reason.[21]

• Fast Breeder Reactors

The belief in earlier postwar decades that the global supply of uranium would be inadequate to meet future demand led to the development of reactors that produce more fissile material than they consume, known as breeder reactors. Surplus plutonium production is achieved in these reactors by surrounding the plutonium fuel with fertile U-238. The U-238 is transmuted to Pu-239 in the fission process.[22]

The United States, the United Kingdom, and Germany have all abandoned the use of breeder technology.[23] France, the world leader in the development of breeder reactors, recently decided not to relicense the world's only commercial-scale breeder, the Superphenix. Russia, Japan, and India, however, continue to be active in the field.

The fast breeder reactor

- has no moderator (in the case of the Liquid Metal Fast Breeder Reactor and the Gas-cooled Fast Reactor)
- uses Pu-239 and U-238 as fuel
- yields 10–40 percent more fissile material than it consumes
- is shut down for refueling

Breeder reactors are of proliferation concern because weapons-usable plutonium is present at all stages of fuel handling and because of their production of surplus plutonium. A 1,000-MW plant typically contains 5,000–6,000 kg of plutonium in its core, and yields 200 kg of plutonium each year.[24] For every Liquid Metal Fast Breeder Reactor in operation, about 2,500 kg of plutonium are being processed, stored, or transported at any moment. Compared to the 250 kg of plutonium discharged from one gigawatt-year's operation of a standard LWR, the breeder reactor is responsible for the production of tremendous quantities of fissile material, which can be used as fuel for another reactor or, conceivably, in a nuclear bomb.[25]

NOTES

1. David Albright, "Civilian Inventories of Plutonium and Highly Enriched Uranium," in Paul Leventhal and Yonah Alexander, eds., *Preventing Nuclear Terrorism* (Lexington, Mass.: Lexington Books, 1987), p. 270.

2. D. Fischer, personal correspondence, May 4, 1992, p. 2.

3. Ibid., p. 3.

4. D. Fischer, personal correspondence, July 15, 1992, p. 4.

5. William C. Potter, *Nuclear Power and Nonproliferation: An Interdisciplinary Perspective* (Cambridge, Mass.: Oelgeschlager, Gunn & Hain, Publishers, 1982), p. 63.

6. Ibid., p. 65.

7. Jacques LeClercq, *The Nuclear Age* (Paris: Le Chene, 1986), p. 71.

8. Ibid., pp. 92–98. This figure does not include RBMK reactors from the former Soviet Union.

9. Anthony Nero, *A Guidebook to Nuclear Reactors* (Berkeley: University of California Press, 1979), p. 91.

10. Ibid., p. 81.

11. D. Fischer, personal correspondence, May 4, 1992, p. 4.

12. William Sweet, *The Nuclear Age: Power, Proliferation, and the Arms Race* (Washington, D.C.: Congressional Quarterly, 1984), p. 41.

13. Nero, p. 116.

14. Nero, p. 114.

15. Potter, p. 66.

16. D. Fischer, personal correspondence, May 4, 1992, pp. 3–4.

17. Ibid., p. 3.

18. Sweet, pp. 39–40.

19. Nero, p. 128.

20. Ibid., p. 126.

21. Joe Bermudez, "North Korea's Nuclear Program," *Jane's Intelligence Review* (September 1991), p. 408.

22. The U-238 absorbs a neutron released by the fission process and becomes U-239, which decays in half an hour to become Np-239 (neptunium). Two days later further decay takes place and the Np-239 becomes Pu-239.

23. Sweet, p. 44.

24. Potter, pp. 68–69.

25. Ibid.

4

The History of the Nonproliferation Regime

U.S. nonproliferation initiatives since World War II have generally promoted increased restrictions on nuclear activities worldwide. These initiatives have helped shape the institutionalized, global effort to control the spread of nuclear weapons known as the nuclear nonproliferation regime. Detailed discussion of various regime elements is provided in the next chapter; the current chapter discusses the evolution of the regime over its nearly fifty-year history, as outlined in Table 4.1.

Table 4.1   Key Events in the History of the Nuclear Nonproliferation Regime

1945	U.S. drops atomic bombs on Hiroshima and Nagasaki
1946	U.S. adopts McMahon Act; proposes internationalist Baruch Plan
1949	USSR tests a nuclear explosive
1952	Great Britain tests a nuclear explosive
1953	U.S. proposes Atoms for Peace
1957	IAEA is founded
1960	France tests a nuclear explosive
1963	Limited Test Ban Treaty is signed
1964	China tests a nuclear explosive
1967	Treaty of Tlatelolco is completed
1968	NPT is completed
1971	Zangger Committee is formed
1974	India tests a nuclear explosive
1975	Nuclear Suppliers Group is created
1978	U.S. Nuclear Non-Proliferation Act is passed
1985	Treaty of Rarotonga is completed
1992	NSG adopts full-scope safeguards export policy, expands trigger list to include dual-use items
	China and France accede to the NPT
1993	North Korea threatens to withdraw from the NPT

EARLY APPROACHES TO NONPROLIFERATION

In the immediate postwar period, U.S. nonproliferation policy followed two opposite tracks. The first, expressed in the 1946 Atomic Energy Act (McMahon Act), relied on government control and secrecy in the nuclear sector to keep nuclear technology, materials, and know-how under U.S. control. On the domestic front, the legislation nationalized all aspects of U.S. nuclear ventures, from uranium mining to nuclear fuel production to the innocuous production of isotopes for medical use. Internationally, it outlawed U.S. export of nuclear materials, technology, and know-how. Even the United Kingdom, the closest wartime partner of the United States in nuclear research, was denied continued collaboration after the war ended. In short, the initial U.S. postwar nonproliferation policy was simple: to stop the spread of nuclear weapons before it started by maintaining tight government control over all nuclear activity in the United States.

A quite different approach to nonproliferation policy, known as the Baruch Plan, was unveiled in mid-1946 by President Truman. The plan was an amended version of a report by Assistant Secretary of State Dean Acheson and Tennessee Valley Authority Chairman David Lilienthal, and it essentially called for the internationalization of all nuclear activities. All but the smallest nuclear facilities worldwide would fall under the management, if not ownership, of an International Atomic Development Authority (IADA), which would also inspect and license nuclear activities and promote the development of nuclear power for peaceful purposes. Most remarkably, the plan envisioned the end of nuclear weapons development and production and the elimination of all atomic weapons stockpiles. The plan had teeth, too: UN-sponsored sanctions were authorized for violators, and these sanctions could not be vetoed in the UN Security Council.[1]

The Baruch Plan, however, was too bold for its day. The former Soviet Union viewed it as a U.S. scheme to maintain U.S. nuclear dominance by freezing its position as the only nation capable of building an atomic bomb. The Soviets were also wary of the plan's enforcement provisions, particularly the no-veto clause, a Baruch contribution to the original Acheson-Lilienthal recommendations that would have prohibited a Security Council veto of its provisions. The Soviet counterproposal to the plan called for the destruction of all nuclear weapons by the United States *before* the establishment of an international control system—the reverse order of business envisioned by the Baruch Plan. In the end, the United States and the Soviet Union could not reconcile their differences, and the plan was dropped. Meanwhile, the restrictive Atomic Energy Act of 1946 remained in place as official U.S. policy until December 1953.

Why the United States simultaneously pursued two divergent nonproliferation policies is debated by scholars to this day. Some allege that the nationalistic Atomic Energy Act represented the "real" U.S. policy: to preserve a U.S. nuclear monopoly as long as possible. The Baruch Plan, they assert, was merely a propaganda effort deliberately designed to be rejected by the Soviet Union. Other scholars describe the Atomic Energy Act as an interim measure that would protect U.S. nuclear secrets until a viable international nuclear control regime based on the Baruch Plan could be worked out.[2] Whatever the truth, the opposing impulses of denial and cooperation—presented in their extreme forms in these postwar policies— have influenced debates on nuclear nonproliferation policy ever since.

In failing to adopt the Baruch Plan, the United States and the former Soviet Union allowed a rare opportunity for the creation of a potent nonproliferation regime to pass. This is especially clear when core elements of the Baruch Plan are compared with those of today's nuclear nonproliferation regime.[3] Where the proposed IADA would have managed or owned all nuclear facilities, today's International Atomic Energy Agency presence in nuclear facilities is limited to on-site technologies and periodic visits needed to fulfill its safeguards obligations. Where the Baruch Plan foresaw the complete elimination of nuclear weapons, today's regime seeks at best to give timely warning of the spread of sensitive nuclear technology. Finally, the bold enforcement capability in the Baruch Plan is replaced today by the IAEA's option to impose its own discipline on an errant member-state[4] or to alert the UN Security Council of suspected violations of a state's commitments under the Non-Proliferation Treaty (NPT). Although today's nuclear nonproliferation regime continues to grow in strength, it is unlikely to encompass in the near future the sweeping measures and global authority envisioned by some U.S. policymakers in 1946.

NUCLEAR PROMOTION THROUGH THE ATOMS FOR PEACE PROGRAM

By 1953, evidence of the failure of the U.S. policy of nuclear secrecy was mounting. The former Soviet Union and the United Kingdom had each tested nuclear explosives, and France and the Netherlands were forging ahead on civil nuclear programs.[5] The U.S. refusal to allow the spread of nuclear technology and know-how, codified in the 1946 Atomic Energy Act, had served to block U.S. participation in the rapidly developing international nuclear market.[6] U.S. fears of increased Soviet influence worldwide through displacement of the United States as the chief supplier of nuclear assistance prompted a reevaluation of U.S. nuclear policy and led to the creation of the Atoms for Peace program.[7]

Atoms for Peace represented a compromise between the Baruch Plan's promise of access to nuclear technology and the McMahon Act's concern for restricting such access. The new policy, proposed in December 1953,

sought to facilitate the dissemination of nuclear energy for peaceful purposes to all interested nations in return for their acceptance of safeguards
against military use of fissile materials. President Eisenhower won high
praise for his new proposal, and the era of nuclear promotion was born. In
only three years, from 1956 to 1959, the United States concluded nuclear cooperation agreements with forty nations, all of whom agreed to allow U.S.
inspectors to monitor technology provided by the United States.[8] These bilateral agreements paved the way for early U.S. dominance of international
nuclear transactions. Between 1956 and 1962, Atoms for Peace provided research reactors, training, and fissile materials to twenty-six nations, including thirteen in developing countries.[9] No uranium enrichment or plutonium
reprocessing plants were included in Atoms for Peace exchanges.

Safeguards did not cover all global nuclear transactions in the 1950s,
however, and the seeds for some of today's proliferation concerns were
sown in that decade. Other nations with advanced nuclear technology, including Canada, France, Great Britain, and the former Soviet Union,
joined the United States in marketing nuclear wares overseas, frequently
without adequate guarantees of their peaceful use.[10] In 1956 Canada sold
a research reactor to India, and the United States supplied heavy water for
the facility, which was not subject to inspections.[11] This reactor, along
with technology for a plutonium reprocessing facility supplied by the
United States and Great Britain in the 1950s and 1960s, produced the plutonium used by India for its 1974 nuclear explosion.[12] France's nuclear export activity was still more imprudent: France deliberately assisted an Israeli nuclear weapons program by selling Tel Aviv a research reactor and
plutonium reprocessing plant. Outside the commercial arena, the former
Soviet Union assisted China with development of its nuclear program in
the late 1950s, providing it with uranium, information on uranium enrichment, and even nuclear weapon design information.[13]

President Eisenhower's Atoms for Peace address to the United Nations in December 1953 called for the creation of what has become the
most visible international agency in the nonproliferation regime—the International Atomic Energy Agency. The IAEA, eventually founded in
1957 as an autonomous agency of the United Nations family, was charged
with assisting the dissemination of nuclear energy for peaceful purposes,
promoting nuclear safety, and administering a system of international nuclear safeguards. The first and second tasks are accomplished by making
technical and safety assistance available to member-states and by cooper-
ating with national and international organizations in novel applications of
nuclear science, such as the use of nuclear isotopes in the fields of medicine and agriculture. The second task involves provision of nuclear safeguards to bilateral or multilateral transfers of nuclear goods and, since
1970, provision of the same service to the entire peaceful nuclear sectors
of NPT non–nuclear weapon states.

A BROADENING CONSENSUS ON NONPROLIFERATION

By the early 1960s, several global developments were creating favorable conditions for completion of arms control and nonproliferation agreements. The development of long-range rockets—dramatically demonstrated in 1957 with the launching of the Sputnik satellite—underlined the vulnerability of both the United States and the former Soviet Union to nuclear attack.[14] Environmental hazards caused by nuclear testing in the atmosphere mobilized public opinion against unrestricted efforts to build bigger and better nuclear weapons. Above all, the Cuban missile crisis drove home the very real possibility of an all-out nuclear exchange.

At the same time, the nuclear club was growing steadily. France conducted its first atomic test in 1960, and China followed suit in 1964. Shortly after the Chinese blast, India began to insist on its right to develop nuclear explosives "for peaceful purposes" and undertook construction of the infrastructure needed to do so.[15] In addition, Germany and Japan were gaining the technological competence needed to build a nuclear bomb—an unnerving prospect for other nations with vivid memories of World War II. Moreover, orders for a new technology—the nuclear power plant—began to roll in and were expected to soar by the end of the decade.[16] Plutonium-bearing spent fuel from these plants would accumulate rapidly in the years ahead, and could encourage non–nuclear weapon states to take the nuclear weapons plunge.

In this context, several steps were taken to strengthen the nonproliferation regime in the 1960s. The Limited Test Ban Treaty (LTBT), concluded in 1963, prohibited nuclear testing on land or in the atmosphere, although underground testing was allowed to continue. The LTBT was a significant achievement in the history of arms control, but was more effective in stopping the spread of nuclear weapons to non–nuclear weapon states ("horizontal proliferation") than it was in slowing the growth of nuclear stockpiles in nuclear weapon states ("vertical proliferation"). France and China, for example, refused to sign, and the former Soviet Union and the United States continued to test underground.

Latin American nations took the lead in creating the next important element in the growing nonproliferation regime—the Treaty on the Prohibition of Nuclear Weapons in Latin America (commonly known as the Treaty of Tlatelolco). Impelled by the Cuban missile crisis, the nations of South and Central America agreed to establish the world's first nuclear weapon–free zone in an area with significant population. The 1967 accord not only forbids the acquisition or development of nuclear weapons in Latin America, but also prohibits their deployment there by foreign powers.

More or less concurrently with the Tlatelolco negotiations in Latin America, the United States, the Soviet Union, and Great Britain began discussions on a global nonproliferation treaty, which was to become the backbone of the nuclear nonproliferation regime. The proposed Nuclear Non-Proliferation Treaty pushed the regime back in the direction of restrictions, away from the relative looseness of the Atoms for Peace era. The nuclear powers involved in negotiating the NPT sought formal commitments by non–nuclear weapon states not to pursue development of nuclear weapons, nor to obtain them from other nations, and to safeguard their nuclear material and nuclear exports.

Non–nuclear weapon nations made several demands of their own. Some sought assurances that nuclear weapon states would work toward specific disarmament goals. Others wanted "negative security assurances," that is, commitments by nuclear nations never to target nonnuclear nations for nuclear attack. Still others sought assistance in the development of atomic power for peaceful purposes. Industrial nonnuclear nations sought to ensure that the proposed nonproliferation treaty would not give the nuclear nations a competitive advantage in nuclear commerce.

Two bargains were struck to reconcile opposing nuclear positions and complete the treaty. First, the treaty was written to affirm the right of any nation to develop nuclear energy for peaceful purposes, and it proposes technical assistance to this end. In return, non–nuclear weapon states agree not to develop nuclear weapons and to accept safeguards on their peaceful nuclear activities and on their exports. Second, the treaty requires nuclear powers to move toward disarmament, although it sets no deadlines for reaching specific disarmament objectives. (To pressure nuclear powers for compliance in this area, the treaty was not written to be of indefinite duration; it provides that a conference be called in 1995 to examine its extension.) With the nonproliferation, disarmament, and access questions addressed, the NPT was completed in 1968 and entered into force in 1970.

THE EVOLUTION OF NUCLEAR EXPORT CONTROLS

The 1970s was a decade of regime solidification, as nations moved to tighten up recently established rules in response to several international nuclear developments.[17] The most jolting of these events was the 1974 Indian atomic blast, labeled a "peaceful nuclear explosion" by the Indian government, which brought home in dramatic fashion the problem of the potential global spread of nuclear weapons. For governments that had grown complacent about proliferation problems after completion of the NPT, the Indian development served as a clear signal that much work remained to be done in the nonproliferation arena.

The second major event influencing the regime in the 1970s was the fourfold rise in oil prices in 1973. Nuclear power became an increasingly attractive alternative to oil, and because uranium was believed to be relatively scarce, plutonium-fueled nuclear plants were becoming favored. In fact, the IAEA projected that plutonium fuel would be in use in forty nations by the end of the 1980s.[18] The challenge of ensuring that large quantities of separated plutonium—weapons-usable material—was not put to military use was expected to be a formidable one for the regime.

Third, an increasing number of nations were demonstrating interest in plutonium reprocessing.[19] Even under international safeguards, reprocessing is of high proliferation concern: a nation could divert safeguarded weapons-usable plutonium from a reprocessing plant to a waiting bomb design in a relatively short period, allowing the international community little time to organize an effective response. Several nations appeared to look to a nuclear explosive capability (and indirectly, to sensitive nuclear facilities) to improve their position in a deteriorating regional security environment:

- Pakistan, spurred by the Indian explosion, accelerated efforts to acquire a plutonium reprocessing plant from France, and to develop a secret uranium enrichment program.[20]
- Taiwan, seeking to strengthen its position vis-à-vis the People's Republic of China (PRC), also asked France for reprocessing technology, and later requested the United Kingdom to reprocess Taiwanese spent fuel and return the extracted plutonium to Taiwan.
- South Korea, fearing its neighbor to the north and unsure of the U.S. commitment to its defense in the wake of the Vietnam War, sought reprocessing technology from France.[21]
- Iraq, responding to perceived threats from Israel and Iran, geared up for both a uranium enrichment and a plutonium reprocessing capability.[22]
- South Africa, concerned about the Soviet and Cuban presence on the continent, built a uranium enrichment plant in the mid-1970s and developed weapons-grade enriched uranium from it by the early 1980s.[23]

These developments, along with imprudent exports by the nuclear supplier states (such as the 1975 West German contract with Brazil for technology covering the entire nuclear fuel cycle), led to measures designed to fortify the nonproliferation structures established in the 1960s. Three of these structures are described below.

• Zangger Committee

The NPT requires that nuclear "equipment or material" be under safeguards after export to a non–nuclear weapon state.[24] To ensure consensus on the interpretation of this clause, a committee representing more than a dozen nuclear exporting nations was formed in 1971 to draw up a specific "trigger list" of nuclear materials and technologies that would require IAEA safeguards as a condition of export. The formal list, which included reprocessing plants and enrichment equipment among other items, was communicated to the IAEA in 1974. The Zangger list is significant as the first major agreement by nuclear exporters on the regulation of nuclear trade. The group's membership was limited, however: France, India, and the PRC chose not to participate.[25] (See Chapter 5, Legal Structures, for a list of members.)

• The Nuclear Suppliers Group

The Indian explosion and the expected growth in nuclear facilities world-wide prompted a reappraisal of the adequacy of export controls and led to the establishment in 1975 of the Nuclear Suppliers Group (or London Club) to consider further restrictions on nuclear trade. Membership in the NSG was similar to that of the Zangger Committee, but also included France, a major nuclear exporter, which as a nonparty to the NPT was not part of the Zangger group.

The NSG succeeded in bringing order and major-supplier consensus to nuclear trade by establishing in 1977 a common set of voluntary standards for international nuclear transfers to non–nuclear weapon states. These standards included strict security arrangements covering nuclear exports, a requirement of consent from the original supplier of trigger list items for reexport of the item, and most important, "restraint" in the export of sensitive technology such as uranium enrichment and plutonium reprocessing plants. (In effect, this restraint has constituted nearly a complete embargo.) Formation of the NSG reflected increasing agreement among major suppliers of the need to restrict sensitive nuclear exports. However, the group was viewed by developing nations as a cartel intent on limiting their nuclear development potential.

• The Nuclear Non-Proliferation Act

Although the work of the Zangger Committee and the London Club helped define the trade restrictions in the NPT's Article III.2, significant gaps in the nuclear export control regime continued to allow nations in pursuit of a nuclear weapon to obtain sensitive nuclear materials legally. For example, the NPT, the Zangger Committee, and the London Club all required the relatively lax item-only safeguards as a condition of nuclear export. Under this system, an importing nation agrees to place a particular nuclear import under international safeguards; other nuclear technology or material in the importing nation does not require safeguards. A stricter system, based on full-scope safeguards, requires safeguards on *all* nuclear facilities in the importing nation before the nation can accept nuclear imports. The absence of an extensive full-scope safeguards system in the 1970s allowed Brazil, for example, to transfer to indigenous Brazilian nuclear facilities the knowledge gained from operating imported West German nuclear hardware. These unsafeguarded facilities were dedicated to development of a nuclear weapons capability.

The U.S. Congress and the Carter administration, aware of this and other loopholes and concerned about the attractiveness of the plutonium fuel cycle for many nations, introduced the most restrictive U.S. nuclear policy since the 1946 McMahon Act. President Carter reaffirmed President Ford's election eve announcement that the United States would no longer reprocess spent fuel or export enrichment or reprocessing technology.[26] He also attempted to defer commercialization of breeder reactors in the United States, arguing that uranium stocks were sufficient to supply the nuclear world until a safe fuel cycle was developed in the next century to support the breeder.[27] (The Congress overruled the president on this point, but eventually did kill the demonstration breeder at Clinch River.)

Meanwhile, the Congress was laboring over a new nonproliferation bill, and worked with the Carter administration to produce the Nuclear Non-Proliferation Act (NNPA) of 1978. This tough and comprehensive legislation provided for:

- an end to nuclear trade with non–nuclear weapon states whose nuclear facilities were not subject to full-scope safeguards
- a requirement of U.S. permission for the reprocessing, enrichment, or re-export of nuclear materials received from the United States (known as "prior consent")[28]
- a prohibition on nuclear exports to non–nuclear weapon states that detonate a nuclear device
- the renegotiation of existing supply contracts to meet these conditions[29]

The shift in U.S. nonproliferation policy was unpopular abroad. With the exception of Canada and Australia, U.S. allies were upset about what appeared to be a unilateral attempt by the United States to change the rules of nuclear trade. The Europeans and Japanese strongly—and successfully— resisted the Carter administration attempts to persuade them to abandon their domestic reprocessing and breeder reactor programs.[30] Most were more dependent on nuclear power than was the United States and viewed the breeder reactor as an important part of their long-term energy strategy. Some even accused the United States of seeking to undermine international confidence in breeder and reprocessing technologies in order to eliminate the technological lead that other nations had taken in these fields.

Today, however, much of the Carter-era nonproliferation policy has been vindicated. Uranium is plentiful and breeders are uneconomical, corroborating the U.S. position that a commitment to a plutonium fuel cycle could be deferred. Full-scope safeguards as a condition of export are now standard practice for most nuclear supplier nations, and the sale of sensitive facilities, even under safeguards, is virtually unheard of among the traditional suppliers. Although the Carter policy is criticized for having used too unilateral an approach, its provisions are increasingly accepted as the global standards for nonproliferation policy.

CONCERN ABOUT "THRESHOLD STATES"

During the 1980s, new patterns of sensitive nuclear technology acquisition began to appear, which posed significant challenges for the regime. Whereas Argentina, Brazil, India, Israel, and Pakistan previously had approached large nuclear firms (often openly) to purchase entire sensitive facilities for their civil nuclear power programs, the 1980s nuclear aspirant typically shopped for dual-use components from underground sources in a more secretive, piecemeal attempt to develop a nuclear explosive capability. The export controls of the Zangger Committee and the Nuclear Suppliers Group were significant advances for the regime, but they were not designed to deal with this approach to nuclear weapons development, and the nuclear programs of several nations advanced in spite of the 1970s-era controls. India, for example, apparently received Norwegian and Russian heavy water originally bound for Europe, and Iraq's nuclear program profited from components supplied by German, Swiss, British, and French firms.

In the United States, the Nuclear Non-Proliferation Act of 1978 continued to be the centerpiece of nonproliferation policy, but the Reagan administration was more selective in applying it than the Carter administration had been. Reagan favored a relaxation of restrictions for (1) nations with advanced nuclear programs of no proliferation concern, and (2) nations of strategic significance to the United States. A more flexible and politically pragmatic policy, the Reagan approach nevertheless opened the door to new proliferation problems.

An example of the more flexible U.S. policy toward advanced nuclear nations was the termination of U.S. efforts to discourage European and Japanese development of a fast breeder reactor or fuel reprocessing. In 1988 the Reagan administration exempted Japan from the long-standing U.S. requirement that Japan obtain U.S. permission each time it sought to reprocess U.S.-origin nuclear fuel or to have it reprocessed abroad.[31] Japan was granted advance consent for reprocessing and shipment activities for thirty years, thus eliminating an important source of U.S. control over the movement or accumulation of sensitive nuclear materials.[32]

Flexibility of U.S. nonproliferation policy toward a strategic ally is best illustrated in the case of U.S.-Pakistani relations in the 1980s. Since the mid-1970s the U.S. government had worried that Pakistan was intent on gaining a nuclear weapons capability, and thus cut off aid to the South Asian nation in 1977 and 1979 to express disapproval of the Pakistani movement in this direction. When the former Soviet Union invaded Afghanistan in 1979, however, Pakistan's value as a strategic asset led the United States to turn a blind eye to Pakistani nuclear activities. The Reagan administration asked the Congress to exempt Pakistan from the U.S. law stipulating termination of assistance to non–nuclear weapon states that import sensitive nuclear facilities, and to approve $3.2 billion in aid to Pakistan in 1981. The lenient U.S. policy toward Pakistan in the 1980s undoubtedly facilitated the Pakistani nuclear program by removing important disincentives to the development of a nuclear arsenal.

Another challenge to the regime in the 1980s was the 1981 Israeli bombing of a nuclear reactor under construction in Iraq. The bombing set back Iraq's probable pursuit of a nuclear bomb, but it also signaled a lack of confidence in international nuclear safeguards. Ironically, an NPT signatory (Iraq), allegedly cheating on the treaty by pursuing development of a nuclear weapon, was deterred not by safeguards but by military action from a non-NPT nation (Israel). Both the alleged Iraqi program and the Israeli response to it were proof, some argued, that little faith could be placed in the NPT and the international safeguards system.

Not all the nonproliferation news in the 1980s was dismal, however. In the South Pacific a new nonproliferation treaty, the Treaty of Rarotonga, was signed. It contains provisions not found in the NPT nor in the Treaty of Tlatelolco, such as the requirement that some exports to nuclear weapon states be safeguarded. However, because only Australia (already an NPT party) has a nuclear facility of any significance among treaty parties, and because uranium is the region's only significant nuclear export, the treaty has had little immediate impact on the area.[33] Still, by seeking a nuclear free zone in the South Pacific, and particularly because it borders on similar zones in Latin America and Antarctica, the treaty served to revive interest in the contribution of such zones to peace.

In addition, Argentina and Brazil, rival nations believed to be pursuing their own nuclear weapons capabilities, began to undertake confidence-building measures in 1985 to assure each other of the peaceful intent of their nuclear programs.

Finally, leading nations in the nonproliferation regime began to address the advancing capability of many nations to deliver warheads of mass destruction over long distances. Canada, France, Italy, Japan, the United Kingdom, the United States, and West Germany established the Missile Technology Control Regime in 1987 to control the spread of missile-related technologies. Spain, Belgium, Luxembourg, and the Netherlands joined in 1989 and 1990, and the USSR, Sweden, and Switzerland all agreed to abide by its provisions.[34]

NEW RECRUITS AND NEW STRENGTH FOR THE NONPROLIFERATION REGIME

Several developments in the early 1990s led to a significant strengthening of the nonproliferation regime. Regime rules were tightened, and nations long outside the regime decided to embrace it. Two geopolitical developments—the end of the Cold War and the outbreak of the Gulf War—were especially influential in shaping the regime by focusing global attention on regime loopholes and inspiring action to close them.

• The Cold War

Ironically, nonproliferation policy was one area in which the United States and the Soviet Union cooperated closely during much of the Cold War. The two superpowers found common cause in preventing the spread of nuclear explosives to other nations, even as they bitterly disputed a host of other issues. Today, the former Soviet Union is itself a cause of proliferation concern, and Moscow's ability to influence other governments on proliferation issues is greatly diminished.

The emergence of newly independent, non-Russian republics with nuclear weapons on their territories, ambivalent attitudes toward proliferation issues, and little or no experience in the administration of export controls leads many to fear a hemorrhaging of nuclear materials, technology, and know-how from the former Soviet Union. The economic crises in many of the republics make this concern even more acute: the sale of sensitive nuclear goods may be one of the few options open to many struggling governments to earn hard currency.

Concern about these issues inspired action in 1991 and 1992 to prevent the envisioned proliferation nightmares. The U.S. Congress appropriated funding in 1991 to assist in the safe dismantlement of Russian nuclear weapons. In addition, the United States, the European Community, France, and Canada established scientific centers in 1992 in selected former Soviet republics to provide meaningful work for scientists in an effort to discourage their emigration to nations of proliferation concern.

• The Gulf War

The second major geopolitical event of the 1990s, the Gulf War, served to strengthen the nonproliferation regime in several ways. First, the revelation of Iraq's clandestine nuclear activity, which violated its commitments as an NPT signatory, shocked much of the world and led to strengthened inspections authority for the International Atomic Energy Agency. Member-states voted in February 1992 to encourage the agency to make greater use of its special inspections power, which allows the agency to enter and scrutinize, outside the routine inspections schedule, nuclear facilities in nations suspected of having or using fissile material in violation of its safeguards agreements.

Second, Iraq's ability to acquire sensitive technologies led to a strengthened export controls commitment on the part of nuclear suppliers worldwide. At their April 1992 meeting, members of the Nuclear Suppliers Group agreed to make full-scope safeguards a condition of export, and expanded the list of materials and technologies triggering these safeguards to include dual-use items, that is, items that could be dedicated to either peaceful or military nuclear uses. As a result of these actions, the undetected export of sensitive nuclear technology and materials is increasingly difficult.

• New Recruits

In the 1990s, a variety of nations have moved to embrace the norms of the nonproliferation regime. The list of signatories to the Non-Proliferation Treaty has continued to grow, with the significant addition of South Africa in July 1991, and the PRC in May 1992. France, the only nuclear weapon state not to accede to the treaty, gained parliamentary approval of such a move in June 1992. The decision by Belarus, Kazakhstan, and Ukraine to accede to the treaty as non–nuclear weapon states avoided a possible crisis for the NPT.

Progress outside the NPT framework is also evident. Brazil and Argentina continue to reject accession to the treaty, but they nevertheless have made major strides toward "transparency" in their nuclear programs. In 1990, Brazil revealed and then terminated a program dedicated to development of nuclear explosives, and the two nations have worked with the IAEA to safeguard their nuclear material. In addition, Argentina agreed in 1992 to abide by the export control practices of the Nuclear Suppliers Group. Finally, Pakistan and India have taken the modest but significant step of agreeing not to attack each other's nuclear facilities.

Interestingly, in many cases a deteriorating security environment originally led these nations to pursue a nuclear weapons capability, and an improved environment appears to explain, at least in part, their rejection of this option. South Africa no longer faces Cuban or Soviet-backed forces in Africa. Brazil and Argentina, both now under civilian governments, have little reason to fear aggression from each other. The withdrawal of U.S. nuclear weapons from South Korea and the North and South Korea joint declaration making the peninsula a nuclear weapon–free zone appear to have given North Korea the confidence to abandon its nuclear aspirations.

CHALLENGES FOR THE FUTURE

The nonproliferation regime is stronger today than at any time in its fifty-year history. The increasing acceptance of restrictive export policies and of strong international safeguards makes the possibility of sensitive nuclear materials acquisition by would-be nuclear powers more and more remote.

Still, the regime faces strong challenges. In the short term, non–nuclear weapon states must be convinced of their stake in the health of the regime, so that the NPT extension conference in 1995 is successful in securing lengthy extension of the Non-Proliferation Treaty. In the long term, governments must acknowledge that most elements of the nonproliferation regime serve at best to buy time. Strict export controls and strong safeguards, desirable as they are, can postpone but not prevent indigenous development of a nuclear explosive capability. Only internationalization of fissile material production and stocks—an idea rooted in the 1946 Baruch Plan—offers long-term hope for stemming the spread of nuclear explosives.

NOTES

1. William C. Potter, *Nuclear Power and Nonproliferation: An Interdisciplinary Perspective* (Cambridge, Mass.: Oelgeschlager, Gunn & Hain, Publishers, 1982), p. 36.

2. Ian Smart, "The Defective Dream," in Joseph F. Pilat, Robert E. Pendley, and Charles K. Ebinger, eds., *Atoms for Peace: An Analysis After Thirty Years*, Westview Special Studies in International Relations (Boulder, Colo.: Westview Press, 1985), p. 76.

3. Potter, p. 40.

4. The IAEA could end technical assistance to the member-state, or expel it from the organization.

5. Bertrand Goldschmidt, *The Atomic Complex: A Worldwide Political History of Nuclear Energy* (La Grange Park, Ill.: American Nuclear Society, 1980), pp. 250–251, 253.

6. Lawrence Scheinman, *The International Atomic Energy Agency and World Nuclear Order* (Washington, D.C.: Resources for the Future, 1987), p. 57.

7. Goldschmidt, p. 253.

8. Ibid., p. 305.

9. Peter R. Mounfield, *World Nuclear Power* (London: Routledge, 1991), p. 41.

10. Leonard S. Spector, *A Historical and Technical Introduction to the Proliferation of Nuclear Weapons* (Washington, D.C.: Carnegie Endowment for International Peace, 1992), p. 10.

11. Ibid., p. 11.

12. Ibid., p. 13.

13. Ibid., p. 16.

14. William Sweet, *The Nuclear Age: Power, Proliferation, and the Arms Race* (Washington, D.C.: Congressional Quarterly, 1984), p. 104.

15. Spector, p. 16.

16. David Fischer, *Stopping the Spread of Nuclear Weapons: The Past and the Prospects* (London: Routledge, 1992), p. 56.

17. Joseph Nye, "Maintaining a Nonproliferation Regime," *International Organization* (Winter 1981), pp. 18–19.

18. Ibid., p. 19.

19. Ibid.

20. Spector, p. 26.

21. Ibid., p. 27.

22. Ibid., p. 28.

23. Ibid.

24. NPT Article III, Paragraph 2.

25. Leonard S. Spector with Jacqueline R. Smith, *Nuclear Ambitions: The Spread of Nuclear Weapons 1989–1990* (Boulder, Colo.: Westview Press, 1990), p. 434.

26. George Rathjens, "Reassessing Nuclear Nonproliferation Policy," *Foreign Affairs* (Spring 1981), p. 878.

27. Joseph Nye, "Nonproliferation: A Long-Term Strategy," *Foreign Affairs* (April 1978), p. 618.

28. Most U.S. nuclear supply agreements already contained prior consent clauses, but the NNPA sought to standardize their application.

29. Potter, p. 48.

30. These technologies have since fallen out of favor in Europe, but the cause was economic rather than U.S. pressure. The French Superphenix breeder reactor, the world's only operating commercial breeder, was refused an extension of its operating license in 1992, essentially killing the project.

31. Tatsujiro Suzuki, "Japan's Nuclear Dilemma," *Technology Review* (October 1991), p. 44.

32. Ibid. p. 45.

33. David Fischer, *The Nuclear Non-Proliferation Regime 1987* (Geneva: United Nations Institute for Disarmament Research), p. 35.

34. Spector and Smith, p. 300.

5

Legal Structures of the Nonproliferation Regime

The nuclear nonproliferation regime is supported by a complex web of treaties, domestic legislation, and export regulations, administered by a host of national and international agencies, which give substance to the norm of nonproliferation. This chapter reviews the contributions of these regime elements to the cause of nonproliferation.

THE CONCEPT OF A REGIME

Theorists of international relations have traditionally thought of global politics in terms of anarchy and conflict. The lack of a political authority that transcends the nation-state has meant that relations in the international system are governed by the "law of the jungle": the strong do what they will, the weak what they can. Thus theorists were increasingly perplexed in the 1970s by certain patterns of increased cooperation among nations. To explain the unusual cooperation, these thinkers developed the notion of an "international regime," a patchwork of institutions, treaties, legislation, and regulations based on shared values and principles. The interaction and mutual reinforcement of these elements, they believed, serve to facilitate cooperation in a particular field, even among nations with an overall history of conflict.[1]

One of the most successful regimes in international politics today is the nuclear nonproliferation regime. The nonproliferation regime is composed of the NPT and the treaties of Tlatelolco and Rarotonga, the International Atomic Energy Agency and various national nuclear control agencies, multilateral export control groups, and domestic legislation and regulations dealing with nuclear control. All are informed to a greater or lesser degree by the shared belief that the spread of nuclear weapons is dangerous for world peace and often constitutes a threat to an individual nation's security.

Largely independent in their creation and operation, the various components of the nonproliferation regime nevertheless overlap and interact with each other in a way that strengthens the norm of nonproliferation. Several nonproliferation treaties, for example, rely on the International Atomic Energy Agency for implementation of their provisions. Nuclear suppliers worldwide cooperate to help define ambiguous sections of the NPT. National nuclear control bureaucracies conform to, and sometimes surpass, the provisions of international treaties. The interconnected nature of the various regime elements serves to strengthen the regime and to defend it against unraveling.

INTERNATIONAL ARRANGEMENTS

• The NPT

The backbone of the effort to control the spread of nuclear weapons is the Treaty on the Non-Proliferation of Nuclear Weapons, commonly called the Non-Proliferation Treaty, or the NPT. Opened for signature in 1968, the treaty entered into force in 1970. No other regime element is more symbolic of nonproliferation or has done more to institutionalize the norm of nonproliferation in foreign ministries and legislatures around the world. Achieving formal commitment by most of the global community not to develop or acquire nuclear weapons was a major advance for the regime. The following discussion of the treaty's weaknesses should not be allowed to overshadow that fact.

Treaty parties. To date, more than 150 nations are party to the NPT, making it the most widely observed arms control agreement in history. Still, omissions from the treaty's signatory list are notable. Israel, which has an extensive nuclear arsenal, and India and Pakistan, which are capable of building nuclear weapons, have refused to sign, as have Argentina and Brazil, although these two have recently taken steps to boost international confidence in the peaceful objectives of their nuclear programs. Significant omissions from the ranks of the NPT-designated nuclear weapon states included France and China until 1992, when both changed longstanding policies and signed the treaty.

On the other hand, North Korea declared in March 1993 its intention to leave the treaty, a worrisome development in its effect on the regime at large and on the security situation in East Asia. Other signatories, such as Iraq, have demonstrated a willingness to circumvent the treaty in pursuit of a nuclear weapons capability, and still others, such as Libya and Iran, are suspected of coveting nuclear weapons.

The NPT bargain. At the heart of the NPT is a bargain between nations possessing nuclear weapons and those that do not. Nuclear weapon states (NWS—those nations known to have detonated a nuclear device before 1967) are bound

- not to help non–nuclear weapon states (NNWS) acquire atomic weaponry
- to share nuclear technology for peaceful purposes with interested nations
- to make a sincere effort to reduce the level of their nuclear stockpiles
- to require that their nuclear exports to NNWS be safeguarded

Non–nuclear weapon states, for their part, agree

- not to pursue the acquisition or development of nuclear weapons
- to place safeguards on their nuclear exports to NNWS
- to accept safeguards on all their nuclear materials, whether imported or indigenously produced (full-scope safeguards)
- to share nuclear technology for peaceful purposes with interested nations

This "safeguards-for-assistance" bargain brought together disparate groups of nations with varying nuclear interests (see Chapter 4, History of the Nonproliferation Regime). While the bargain figures significantly in the continuing support for the treaty, that support is increasingly rooted in many states' perception that the NPT serves their security interests.

Treaty provisions. Several provisions of the NPT remain controversial or misunderstood or both. First, the treaty's differing obligations for NWS and NNWS have led some nations to characterize it as fundamentally unjust, particularly because it appears to freeze the nuclear status quo. The lack of significant progress in superpower nuclear arms reductions between 1970 and 1987, even as NNWS parties observed their commitment not to develop nuclear weapons, convinced some nations that the agreement had served to divide the world permanently into nuclear haves and have-nots. The subsequent completion of the U.S.-Soviet Intermediate Nuclear Force (INF) Treaty, the Strategic Arms Reduction Treaty, and the June 1992 U.S.-Russian agreement on radical nuclear arms cuts have not entirely quelled this criticism. If the NPT is still perceived as being unequally implemented in 1995, it could unfavorably affect the terms on which the treaty is extended.

Second, accession to the NPT does not, as widely believed, guarantee against a party's development of a military nuclear capability. Because inspections are usually based on a list of facilities supplied to the IAEA by the treaty party, the party could conceal the existence of a facility producing or containing fissile material by omitting it from the list. Iraq attempted to use this strategy. Alternatively, a signatory could acquire nuclear technology openly and legally, under international safeguards, then announce withdrawal from the treaty (and from the safeguards it requires) as provided in Article X, in order to pursue nuclear weapons development. No nation has chosen this option.

Third, some nations complain that the NPT requires NNWS parties to accept more comprehensive safeguards than those applied to states outside the treaty. Outsiders purchasing nuclear technology or material from an NPT party are required to accept safeguards on the transferred item (and on nuclear material derived from it or produced by it) but not on other nuclear activities unassociated with the transaction, and no safeguards are required if two outsiders trade.[2] By contrast, the NNWS NPT party is required to accept "full-scope" safeguards, which apply to *all* of its nuclear materials, whether imported or indigenously produced. The stricter safeguards requirements for NPT parties may lead some nations to calculate that their interests are better served by not signing the treaty.

Fourth, the treaty is controversial in its recognition of the rights of NNWS to access the "benefits of peaceful nuclear explosions" (PNEs).[3] PNEs are nuclear explosions used for peaceful purposes. In the 1960s and early 1970s, PNEs were thought to be useful in the construction of harbors, canals, and other infrastructure requiring large-scale excavation, although they have never been used for this purpose.[4] Significantly, the NPT does not provide for NNWS access to the nuclear *devices* used in PNEs, only to the benefits of their use under international observation. This language was adopted to ensure that PNEs not become a backdoor route for acquisition of nuclear explosive technology or know-how.

Finally, the NPT is not of indefinite duration. Article X.2 states: "Twenty-five years after the entry into force of the Treaty, a conference shall be convened to decide whether the Treaty shall continue in force indefinitely, or shall be extended for an additional fixed period or periods." The undefined duration of the treaty was a sine qua non for the accession of key potential nuclear states such as West Germany and Italy.[5] Prominent international legal scholars, however, argue that the NPT cannot legally be voted out of existence in 1995, at least not directly. This argument is considered in Chapter 8, The 1995 NPT Extension Conference.

Despite its imperfections, most experts acknowledge that the NPT is the linchpin of the nonproliferation regime. Most of the other regime elements discussed below grew out of the NPT or imitate the treaty's provisions to a great extent. Without the NPT, many of the regime's elements would not exist, and many nations currently proscribed from joining the nuclear club would be free to do so.

• Zangger Committee

The Zangger Committee is one of the regime elements spawned by the NPT. Established in 1971—a year after the NPT's entry into force—by a group of NPT signatories who were also major nuclear suppliers, its purpose was to flesh out the vague requirement of safeguards on exports of nuclear "equipment and material" contained in Article III.2. The committee made two influential statements to this end. First, it determined that full-scope safeguards were not required by Article III.2. Exporters need only ensure that safeguards are arranged for a particular export, rather than for the importing nation's entire nuclear program. This relatively loose interpretation of the safeguards requirement was an attempt to balance the need to prevent nuclear diversions against the interests of nuclear exporters concerned about preserving access to the global nuclear market.

Second, the committee developed a "trigger list," known as the Zangger list, of items of nuclear equipment and material that require safeguards as a condition of export. All twenty-nine Zangger Committee members (see Table 5.1) voluntarily commit themselves not to export trigger list items unless the importer has arranged for international safeguards on them. The committee's informal legal status (it is an ad hoc arrangement not linked to the NPT) makes its interpretation of Article III.2 nonbinding on non–Zangger Committee NPT parties. Nevertheless, the committee's work was recognized by treaty parties at the fourth NPT review conference in 1990, and the Zangger list is widely regarded as a significant contribution to the nonproliferation regime.

Table 5.1   The Nuclear Suppliers Group and the Zangger Committee: Member-States

Australia	Greece	Romania
Austria	Hungary	Russia
Belgium	Ireland	Slovakia
Bulgaria	Italy	Spain
Canada	Japan	South Africa*
Czech Republic	Luxembourg	Sweden
Denmark	Netherlands	Switzerland
Finland	Poland	United Kingdom
France	Norway	United States
Germany	Portugal	

* South Africa is a member of the Zangger Committee only.

• *Nuclear Suppliers Group (London Club)*

The 1974 Indian nuclear blast shocked the West and led the major nuclear suppliers to question the adequacy of the NPT for regulating the flow of nuclear materials and technology. This concern led to the creation of the Nuclear Suppliers Group, or London Club, to further restrict the supply of items that might be used to advance a nonpeaceful nuclear program. The NSG adopted the Zangger Committee's trigger list, and added to it heavy water and heavy-water production plants. The NSG also required export conditions stricter than those specified in the NPT. Nations importing nuclear materials from NSG member-states were now required

- to accept international safeguards on all imported materials and technology and on facilities using or replicating sensitive materials and technology[6]
- to provide physical security for transferred nuclear facilities and materials
- to agree not to retransfer the nuclear materials and technology to third-party countries without the permission of the original exporter (the NSG member) and without agreement from the third country to abide by these same rules[7]
- to pledge not to use the imports to manufacture nuclear explosives

The purpose of these tightened restrictions was to prevent the manufacture of nuclear explosives, and to prevent nuclear explosions, "peaceful" or otherwise, by NNWS. For their part, the NWS pledged to "exercise restraint" in the export of sensitive nuclear technologies, such as plutonium reprocessing, uranium enrichment, or heavy-water production equipment.[8] In effect, this restraint has amounted to an unofficial embargo on the export of these items—at least at the governmental level—since 1977.[9] One exception to this embargo should be noted: the sale to Argentina of a heavy-water plant by a Swiss firm. On the other hand, many sensitive technologies have been transferred by private firms from NSG nations without the knowledge of their governments.

In April 1992, the twenty-eight Nuclear Suppliers Group member-states (see Table 5.1) further tightened control over nuclear exports in response to revelations of Iraq's clandestine import of nuclear technology. First, the group expanded its trigger list to include sixty-five dual-use items.[10] Second, it agreed to require full-scope safeguards as a condition of export. Although these measures apply only to new contracts, they will steadily close significant gaps in the export controls regime as pre-1992 contracts are completed. Combined with the full-scope safeguards requirements of the NPT and the Tlatelolco and Rarotonga treaties (see Table 5.2), nearly all nuclear and "potentially nuclear" transactions will soon be covered by full-scope safeguards.

Table 5.2   Safeguards Required by the NPT, the Treaties of Tlatelolco and Rarotonga, and the NSG

	Safeguards Required In-Country (Including Imports)	Safeguards Required on Exports
NPT		
Nuclear Weapon State	none	to NWS: none to NNWS: item-only safeguards
Non–Nuclear Weapon State	full-scope safeguards	to NWS: none to NNWS: item-only safeguards
Treaty of Tlatelolco	full-scope safeguards	none[a]
Treaty of Rarotonga	full-scope safeguards	to NWS: "applicable safeguards" to NNWS: full-scope safeguards
Nuclear Suppliers Group	not applicable	full-scope safeguards

Note: Each entry may describe only the minimum requirements governing a transaction. Other safeguards may apply. For example, the NPT requires "item-only" safeguards on exports to NNWS, but exports to an *NPT* NNWS fall under full-scope safeguards.

[a] However, because most Tlatelolco treaty parties are also party to the NPT, and because the IAEA includes an export safeguards clause in the safeguards agreements of those who are not, all nuclear exports from Tlatelolco treaty signatories are safeguarded.

Still, options for the acquisition of unsafeguarded sensitive nuclear technology are not yet completely foreclosed. Several nations capable of exporting nuclear material and technology remain outside the Nuclear Suppliers Group, including Argentina, Brazil, China, India, Israel, Pakistan, South Africa, and the non-Russian former Soviet republics. Most of these are unlikely to export sensitive nuclear technologies, although China and the former Soviet republics are of concern in this regard.[11]

REGIONAL ARRANGEMENTS

• The Treaty of Tlatelolco

The Treaty of Tlatelolco is one of the significant regime elements that preceded creation of the NPT. Concluded in 1967, the Treaty of Tlatelolco sought to establish the world's first nuclear weapon–free zone in an area with significant population. Like the NPT, the treaty of Tlatelolco prohibits NNWS from acquiring nuclear weapons and requires these states to place their peaceful nuclear activities under safeguards. However, the treaty brings several contributions to the regime that are not found in the NPT. First, the Treaty of Tlatelolco is "of a permanent nature and shall remain in force indefinitely." Although provision is made for a signatory to abandon the treaty, the clear intention is to make Latin America a nuclear weapon–free zone for all time. Consequently, the Treaty of Tlatelolco cannot lapse, as the NPT might in the future.

Second, the treaty does not allow the stationing of nuclear weapons anywhere in its zone of application, whereas the NPT permits nuclear weapons to be deployed in a non–nuclear weapon state as long as they are under the control of the nuclear weapon state that owns them.

Third, the Tlatelolco treaty does not differentiate between NWS and NNWS in the application of its key provisions. The reason is simple— there are no NWS in Latin America—but the effect is significant. Some NNWS argue that the treaty is proof that a solid nonproliferation treaty is possible without introducing the nuclear double standards found in the NPT. Brazil and Argentina, for example, have long refused to accede to the NPT because of its "discriminatory" character, but have shown much more interest in living within the provisions of the Treaty of Tlatelolco. The greater appeal of that treaty's uniform approach to nonproliferation may make it a more adequate model for a regional treaty than the NPT.

The Treaty of Tlatelolco does address nuclear weapon states, however, in two protocols to the treaty. Protocol I requires that nations with territories in the region, three of which are NWS, honor all treaty provisions in those territories. All nations affected by Protocol I (the United Kingdom, the Netherlands, the United States, and France) have signed and ratified it. Protocol II obliges NWS not to use or threaten to use nuclear weapons against Tlatelolco treaty parties. It has been signed by all five NWS (United States, Russia, France, United Kingdom, China).

Fourth, the Tlatelolco treaty introduces a novel approach to enforcement that differs from the approach provided in the NPT. Although both treaties address the issue of unscheduled or "special" inspections, these are more sweeping in the Tlatelolco treaty than in the NPT. The Treaty of Tlatelolco provides that signatories may demand inspection of another treaty party's nuclear facilities at any time and requires that the suspect state cooperate fully with the inspection. Thus, these special inspections are frequently referred to as "challenge inspections." By contrast, the NPT does not refer directly to special inspections (although there is no dispute that the treaty authorizes them), and they lack the "challenge" characteristics of their Tlatelolco counterparts. NPT special inspections are initiated by the IAEA, rather than at the request of another treaty party, and must be negotiated with the state suspected of violating its NPT obligations. If the suspected state refuses to cooperate, the IAEA board of governors can order it to comply. If the state still resists, the IAEA can report the matter to the UN Security Council.

The Tlatelolco treaty brings features to the nonproliferation regime that strengthen it significantly, but the treaty has two chief weaknesses. In practice, however, neither has proved to be significant. First, although the Treaty of Tlatelolco, like the NPT, requires each signatory to accept full-scope safeguards on its peaceful nuclear program, the Latin American treaty does not require safeguards on nuclear *exports*. In practice, however, parties to both treaties safeguard their exports, either because most Tlatelolco treaty parties are also party to the NPT (which requires that exports be safeguarded) or because the IAEA has added an export safeguards clause to its safeguards agreements with non-NPT Tlatelolco treaty parties.

The second weakness of the Treaty of Tlatelolco is its ambiguity regarding peaceful nuclear explosions. Whereas the NPT provides for NNWS access to PNE *services* (rather than devices), the Treaty of Tlatelolco appears to allow parties to carry out PNEs themselves, thereby opening the door to NNWS possession and control of nuclear explosive devices.[12] However, such activity is permissible only in accordance with two other treaty articles: Article 1, which prohibits any treaty party involvement with nuclear weapons, and Article 5, which defines nuclear weapons broadly enough to include any nuclear explosive device, including one used in a PNE.[13] The net effect, in the judgment of the United States and the United Kingdom, is to proscribe any use of PNEs. The issue is not as critical today, however, as it was two decades ago, when PNEs were highly touted as exotic uses of the power of the atom. No nation outside the former Soviet Union has considered the use of PNEs since the mid-1970s.

The Treaty of Tlatelolco enters into force for all of Latin America once all affected nations have signed and ratified the treaty and its protocols, and when each signatory has concluded the relevant safeguards agreement with the IAEA. These conditions have not been met. However, twenty-three nations have opted not to wait for all of Latin America to fall into line. By waiving the entry-into-force provisions of the treaty, these twenty-three Latin American and Caribbean signatories agree to be bound by it, making the treaty effective for the vast majority of the continent. The major Tlatelolco treaty holdout nations are Argentina, which has signed but not ratified the treaty; Brazil and Chile, which have signed and ratified the treaty, but have not waived its entry-into-force provisions; and Cuba, which has yet to sign the treaty. Argentina and Brazil appear to be moving closer to bringing the treaty into effect, and Chile and Cuba have indicated they may sign soon, which would bring a Latin American nuclear weapon–free zone closer to reality.

• The Treaty of Rarotonga

Opened for signature in 1985, the Treaty of Rarotonga declares the creation of a South Pacific nuclear free zone encompassing Australia, New Zealand, Papua New Guinea, and several small South Pacific island nations. The Rarotonga treaty contains prohibitions on the acquisition of nuclear weapons similar to those found in the other major nuclear nonproliferation treaties. It also prohibits the testing or deployment of nuclear weapons and the dumping of nuclear wastes anywhere in a broad expanse of the South Pacific. Although the region is not of high proliferation concern, the treaty strengthens the nonproliferation regime by extending to the South Pacific the nuclear weapon–free zone over Antarctica and the one being created throughout Latin America. Thus a significant portion of the Southern Hemisphere is formally free of nuclear weapons.

The most significant difference between the Treaty of Rarotonga and the NPT or the Treaty of Tlatelolco is the strict safeguards required by the South Pacific treaty. Like its predecessor nonproliferation treaties, it requires full-scope safeguards on the peaceful nuclear activities of all NNWS that are party to the treaty. Unlike the earlier accords, however, the Rarotonga treaty also applies the full-scope safeguard requirement as a condition of export. A Rarotonga treaty signatory will not export nuclear materials or technology unless the importing nation accepts safeguards on all of its peaceful nuclear activities. Furthermore, the treaty extends the requirement for safeguards (although not full-scope) to NWS, requiring them to accept "applicable" safeguards on their imports from Rarotonga treaty signatories. The practical effect of this last requirement is to ensure that all uranium from Australia is safeguarded.

• Euratom

One of the earliest regional components of the nonproliferation regime is the European Atomic Energy Community (Euratom). Euratom was established in 1957 as one of three original pillars of the emerging European Community, and was given safeguarding authority over the nuclear facilities in member-states. Today Euratom shares this responsibility in its NNWS with the IAEA, because of the IAEA's role as the administrator of NPT safeguards. See Chapter 6, International Safeguards, for a more complete discussion of NPT and Euratom safeguards.

The legal characteristics of the NPT, the treaties of Tlatelolco and Rarotonga, Euratom, and the NSG are compared in Table 5.3.

NATIONAL LEGISLATION

Although national legislation has no legal authority internationally, it can play an influential role in strengthening the nonproliferation regime. As leaders of the nonproliferation regime, the United States and the Soviet Union set national nonproliferation policies that influenced the nonproliferation policies and practices of their respective allies. The USSR, for example, required for decades that spent fuel from reactors it supplied abroad be returned to the Soviet Union for disposal. This policy helped to control

Table 5.3 Legal Characteristics of Selected Institutions of the Nonproliferation Regime

	Restrictions on Exports	Restrictions In-Country, Including Imports	Peaceful Nuclear Explosions	Treaty Duration	Inspections
NPT	item-only	NWS: none NNWS: full-scope safeguards	highly restricted[a]	to be extended in 1995	routine, ad hoc, and special inspections are possible[b]
Treaty of Tlatelolco	none[c]	full-scope safeguards	highly restricted[d]	indefinite	routine; provision for "challenge" inspections
Treaty of Rarotonga	to NWS: item-only[e] to NNWS: full-scope safeguards	full-scope safeguards	highly restricted[f]	indefinite	same as for NPT
Euratom	none[b]	full-scope safeguards in Euratom NNWS	prohibited to Euratom NNWS as parties to the NPT	indefinite	same as for NPT
NSG	to NWS: none to NNWS: full-scope safeguards	none	highly restricted		NPT type

Notes:

a The NPT reads that the "benefits of" PNEs should be available to NNWS, implying that the NNWS cannot have control of the nuclear explosive device.

b Routine inspections refer to the normally scheduled inspections negotiated between the IAEA and the state. Ad hoc inspections are those undertaken in the absence of a safeguards agreement between the IAEA and the state. Special inspections are those that take place outside the boundaries (of time or place) set by the IAEA-state safeguards agreement.

c Neither the Treaty of Tlatelolco nor Euratom requires safeguards on exports, but most of their signatories or member-states are parties to the NPT, which does have an export safeguards requirement.

d The Treaty of Tlatelolco explicitly allows for PNEs, but under conditions so restrictive that NWS and some treaty signatories maintain that PNEs are, in effect, illegal.

e The Treaty of Rarotonga refers to these as "applicable" safeguards.

f The Treaty of Rarotonga prohibits the manufacture, acquisition, or control of any nuclear device, for whatever purpose. A PNE service carried out on a party's behalf appears to be possible, however.

tightly the supply of plutonium in nations of the former Eastern bloc. The United States, for decades the world's leading supplier of nuclear technology, wielded enormous influence around the globe through its national legislation, even if other nations were sometimes reluctant to follow its lead. The U.S. Nuclear Non-Proliferation Act of 1978 is a case in point.

• U.S. Nuclear Non-Proliferation Act

In 1978, the U.S. Congress and the Carter administration produced the greatest restrictions on nuclear technology since the early 1950s. Called the Nuclear Non-Proliferation Act, the new policy contained the following provisions:

- It required full-scope safeguards as a condition of U.S. nuclear exports to any NNWS.
- It made illegal the export of nuclear materials or technology to any nation acquiring or attempting to acquire a nuclear explosive device.
- It continued the U.S. ban on the export of reprocessing or enrichment facilities.

The legislation also sought to ban the use of breeder reactors and commercial plutonium reprocessing, both in the United States and abroad. Proponents of breeder reactors and reprocessing equipment (technologies that allow nuclear fuel to be recycled) reasoned that these technologies would provide a perpetual supply of nuclear fuel with a minimum input of fresh uranium and with low levels of nuclear waste. The Carter administration sought to avoid this "closed" nuclear fuel cycle because of the large amounts of plutonium it would create. The measures were controversial in the United States and abroad, with only Canada and Australia solidly in support of the U.S. position. Today, however, many key features of the NNPA, such as the full-scope safeguards requirement and the ban on the export of reprocessing or enrichment facilities, are national policy among the world's principal nuclear suppliers.

OTHER STRUCTURES

• The International Atomic Energy Agency

Founded in 1957 as the centerpiece of President Eisenhower's Atoms for Peace program, the IAEA is the world's most visible intergovernmental nuclear body. Its purposes are twofold: (1) to promote the peaceful uses of nuclear energy and (2) to help safeguard civil nuclear materials against diversion to military use. The first is carried out through technical assistance programs in the fields of nuclear power, nuclear medicine, nuclear applications to agriculture, and other uses of nuclear isotopes. The second role makes the IAEA a pillar of the nonproliferation regime, and is achieved through the administration of a safeguards program to civil nuclear activities in non–nuclear weapon states.

The IAEA is made up of a general conference, a board of governors, and a secretariat.

The general conference. The general conference consists of the entire membership of the IAEA. It meets once annually, usually in September, and is tasked with approving the agency budget, accepting applications for new members, and approving the board of governors' choice of director general. It is also important as a forum for discussion of broad issues of agency policy.

The board of governors. The agency's executive authority rests in the board of governors, a thirty-five–seat committee that typically meets five times annually to give guidance to the director general on budgetary, program, and policy issues. The board's membership rotates annually, as eleven of the twenty-two elected members are chosen by the general conference for two-year terms. The remaining thirteen members serve one-year terms and are designated by the outgoing board under a complex formula, which assures the representation of leading producers of nuclear technology and of nuclear source material from various regions.[14] The formula virtually guarantees these leading producers a permanent seat on the board: the ranks of the designated members have changed only once since the 1960s, when South Africa was replaced by Egypt.

The secretariat. The secretariat is the IAEA's administrative arm, with 695 professional and 1,043 support staff in 1990.[15] It manages agency programs, which are organized under five departments: Technical Cooperation, Nuclear Energy and Safety, Administration, Research and Isotopes, and Safeguards. The chief administrative officer of the agency is the director general, who reports to the board of governors.

Since 1984 the IAEA has operated under a "zero real growth" budget policy. The stagnant budget is of proliferation concern as it coincides with increased worldwide demand for safeguards and inspection services. Inadequate safeguards attention to new nuclear facilities increases the likelihood of an illegal diversion of fissile materials.

NOTES

1. The classic definition of a regime is a set of "principles, norms, rules and decision-making procedures around which actor expectations converge in a given issue area." See Stephen D. Krasner, "Structural Causes and Regime Consequences:

Regimes as Intervening Variables," in Stephen D. Krasner, ed., *International Regimes* (Ithaca, N.Y.: Cornell University Press, 1983).

2. If the traded material had originated in an NPT state, however, or was under safeguards for some other reason, safeguards would continue to follow it.

3. NPT, Article V.

4. Proposals for PNEs in Madagascar, Egypt, Panama, and Malaysia are briefly described in David A.V. Fischer, *The International Non-Proliferation Regime, 1987* (Geneva: United Nations Institute for Disarmament Research, 1987), p. 23.

5. George Bunn, Charles N. Van Doren, and David Fischer, *Options and Opportunities: The NPT Extension Conference of 1995* (Southampton: Programme for Promoting Nuclear Non-Proliferation, 1991), pp. 2–3.

6. Replicated enrichment, reprocessing, and heavy-water production facilities would be safeguarded, whereas nonsensitive replicated facilities, such as a reactor or fuel fabrication plant, would not.

7. William C. Potter, *Nuclear Power and Nonproliferation: An Interdisciplinary Perspective* (Cambridge, Mass.: Oelgeschlager, Gunn & Hain, Publishers, 1982), p. 45.

8. R. Timerbaev, "A Major Milestone in Controlling Nuclear Exports," *Eye on Supply* (Spring 1992).

9. Ibid.

10. Timerbaev, p. 8.

11. David Fischer, "Sorting Out International Safeguards: Treaty Requirements for Safeguards and Nuclear Export Controls," paper prepared for presentation at The Nonproliferation Predicament in the Former Soviet Union, Monterey, Calif., April 6–9, 1992.

12. Article 18 allows contracting parties to "carry out explosions of nuclear devices for peaceful purposes—including explosions which involve devices similar to those used in nuclear weapons."

13. Fischer, *The International Non-Proliferation Regime,* p. 31.

14. Lawrence Scheinman, *The International Atomic Energy Agency and World Nuclear Order* (Washington, D.C.: Resources for the Future, 1987), p. 82.

15. International Atomic Energy Agency, "What Is the IAEA?" (Vienna: IAEA Division of Public Information, n.d.).

6

International Safeguards

Safeguards are the confidence-building tools of the nonproliferation regime. The NPT, the treaties of Tlatelolco and Rarotonga, and the Nuclear Suppliers Group all rely on international safeguards to assure their membership that commitments undertaken by other participating nations are being honored. This chapter further details the international safeguards system introduced in Chapter 5.

THE EVOLUTION OF SAFEGUARDS

Most of today's nuclear safeguards are mandated by the NPT, but safeguards predate the 1970 treaty by more than a decade. Throughout the 1950s the United States administered safeguards on nuclear materials and technology transferred to other nations. In 1957 the European Atomic Energy Community was established and given safeguarding authority over nuclear facilities in the European Community. The same year saw the establishment of the International Atomic Energy Agency, which was granted safeguarding jurisdiction over its own technical assistance projects in member-states, over transferred materials and technology (at the request of the trading parties), and over any other nuclear activities a state may want safeguarded. The first IAEA safeguards, requested in 1958, were applied to uranium in a Japanese research reactor.

By 1961 the IAEA had developed its own model safeguards agreement, intended to standardize the interpretation and application of the safeguards mandate found in its statutes. A 1965 model agreement, called INFCIRC/66 (agency shorthand for "Information Circular 66"), is still used today for some safeguards administered by the IAEA.[1]

INFCIRC/66 relies heavily on inspections to fulfill its safeguards mission and is vague about the details of safeguards administration.[2] In part to correct these perceived deficiencies, a new safeguarding document,

INFCIRC/153, was negotiated in 1970 for use under the NPT, which had recently entered into force. It is also used for Tlatelolco treaty safeguards. Today, INFCIRC/153 is the principal nuclear safeguards model agreement. It differs from INFCIRC/66 in several important ways, which are discussed below and summarized in Table 6.1.

Table 6.1   Characteristics of INFCIRC/66 and INFCIRC/153 Model Safeguards Agreements

	INFCIRC/66	INFCIRC/153
Type	"item-only"—covers particular nuclear technology or material	"full-scope"—all nuclear material in peaceful activities in a nation
Parties affected	(1) nations importing from NPT parties; (2) other importers, as required by exporters	NNWS parties to the NPT and treaties of Tlatelolco and Rarotonga[a]
Focus	nuclear facilities and materials[b]	nuclear materials
Advantages	IAEA access whether covered facilities contain nuclear material or not	safeguards are comprehensive
Disadvantages	applies only to particular facilities; "parallel" program is possible and legal	limited IAEA access to nuclear facility without fissile material

Source: Note b—D. Fischer, personal correspondence, July 9, 1992, p. 9.

[a] INFCIRC/153 will also govern Argentine and Brazilian full-scope safeguards when they go into effect.

[b] Nuclear material may be withdrawn from safeguards by an NPT NNWS for use in "non-explosive" military activities such as submarine propulsion. No NPT NNWS has made use of this right.

In sum, by the 1970s three principal nuclear safeguards agreements were in use around the world: the Euratom accords, IAEA INFCIRC/66, and IAEA INFCIRC/153. Since then, new regional treaties that require the application of safeguards have been negotiated, but most employ safeguards agreements similar or identical to these model documents. The Treaty of Rarotonga, completed in 1986, uses the INFCIRC/153 model agreement for safeguards in its member-states, and the Argentine-Brazilian Agency for Accounting and Control of Nuclear Materials (ABACC), established in 1991, uses safeguarding procedures similar to those used by the IAEA and Euratom in Europe.

GENERAL GOALS OF SAFEGUARDS

A broad statement of safeguards goals can be found in the parent documents of the IAEA and Euratom safeguards agreements. INFCIRC/66 agreements take their inspiration from the IAEA statutes, which authorize agency safeguarding in order to ensure that covered items "are not used in such a way as to further any military purpose." Since the 1974 Indian nuclear blast, all safeguards agreements concluded under INFCIRC/66 further stipulate that safeguarded items may not be used for any nuclear weapon or any other military purpose or for any nuclear explosive.[3]

INFCIRC/153's parent document, the NPT, is a bit less comprehensive on the subject of the purpose of safeguards. NPT safeguards are meant to verify compliance with the treaty "with a view to preventing the diversion of nuclear energy from peaceful uses to nuclear weapons or other nuclear explosive devices." The NPT leaves room for unsafeguarded nonexplosive military uses of nuclear power, such as nuclear propulsion for submarines.

The objective of Euratom safeguards is different. Euratom safeguards are simply intended to verify that nuclear material is being used for the purpose declared by the safeguarded state.[4] In fact, a Euratom member-state could legally use safeguarded fissile material in a nuclear weapons program if it had declared this to be the destination of the material. In practice, however, Euratom safeguards verify the peaceful use of safeguarded material and technology, just as IAEA safeguards do, because all Euratom member-states are also party to the NPT and must comply with the treaty's more restrictive IAEA safeguards.

Despite their differences, the safeguards described above all have an important feature in common. Each is designed to verify compliance with treaty obligations rather than prevent diversion of nuclear material. This important distinction is widely unappreciated and is the source of much unwarranted criticism of the IAEA in particular. The agency has no clandestine intelligence capability, nor is it endowed by member-states with enforcement powers. It uses materials accounting, surveillance, and limited inspections to verify the location and use of fissile material, and the conditions under which these tools are used is strictly defined in negotiations with the state. Safeguards are intended to sound an alarm, not to apprehend the thief, and for this purpose they generally have worked admirably.

To clarify, today's international nuclear safeguards are *not* designed to

- *prevent* a nuclear facility operator from gaining physical access to fissile material or from diverting it to proscribed uses[5]
- *prevent* stockpiling of safeguarded weapons-usable material[6]
- seek out hidden nuclear activity or regulate national nuclear programs[7]
- allow inspectors to roam a nation's territory indiscriminately in search of treaty violations
- provide physical security for safeguarded materials[8]

Instead, they *are* intended to verify that nations are living up to their international obligations. The details of this general objective are discussed next.

SPECIFIC GOALS OF SAFEGUARDS

INFCIRC/66 is ambiguous in key areas; it does not, for example, mention specific safeguarding goals. This shortcoming was corrected in INFCIRC/153, which gives a quantifiable interpretation to the NPT's broadly stated nonproliferation objective. The 153 agreement, which serves as the basis for safeguards under the NPT and the treaties of Tlatelolco and Rarotonga, seeks "the timely detection of diversion of significant quantities of nuclear material from peaceful nuclear activities to the manufacture of nuclear weapons or of other explosive devices, or for purposes unknown, and deterrence of such diversion by the risk of early detection."[9]

Several important clauses of this statement are worthy of further scrutiny:[10]

- *Timely detection* is based on the amount of time needed to convert a particular nuclear material to a weapons-usable form. This measure varies for different nuclear materials and for different stages of processing, and ranges from a few days to a full year.
- *Significant quantities* refers to the amount of nuclear material needed to make a country's first nuclear explosive.[11]
- *Risk of early detection* is the probability that diverted material will be detected. The agency seeks a 90–95 percent probability of early detection with only a 5 percent probability of a false alarm (i.e., falsely concluding, on the basis of accountancy alone, that diversion has occurred).[12]

In short, the IAEA believes it is very likely to detect a diversion of bomb-usable amounts of safeguarded nuclear material within the window of time needed to convert that material into a nuclear explosive. The agency's record in this respect is very good.

WHAT IS SAFEGUARDED?

The question of safeguards coverage can be addressed on three levels: (1) what is the global scope of the safeguards net? (2) what is the national scope of the safeguards net? and (3) what specific items are subject to safeguards? The answers to all three questions depend once again on which safeguards agreement or treaty governs the safeguards in question.

• Global Scope of Safeguards

Most nations party to the three major nonproliferation treaties, some of their trading partners, and a few unrelated nations are covered to one degree or another by international nuclear safeguards. The NPT and the treaties of Tlatelolco and Rarotonga all require that non–nuclear weapon state signatories safeguard all nuclear material used for peaceful purposes within their borders.

The NPT also requires that nuclear *exports* from all treaty parties to non–nuclear weapon states be safeguarded. In this way, even non-NPT signatories are affected by the NPT if they import nuclear material or facilities from an NPT party. The Treaty of Rarotonga duplicates this export safeguards requirement and extends it to cover nuclear weapon states as well. Finally, Euratom member-states have their own safeguards requirements.

Outside of formal treaty structures, nuclear suppliers may also require safeguards on transferred nuclear items. (Safeguards requirements of the three major nonproliferation treaties are explained in Chapter 5, Legal Structures of the Nonproliferation Regime.)

Nuclear weapon states are not subject to the comprehensive safeguards required of NNWS under the NPT and the Treaty of Rarotonga because detecting diversion of NWS fissile material to nuclear explosives would be expected and pointless.

• National Scope of Safeguards

The two INFCIRC safeguards documents and the Euratom accords require different ranges of safeguards coverage within a nation. INFCIRC/153 is a full-scope accord: its safeguards apply to *all* nuclear materials declared by a nation to be used for peaceful purposes, whether these are imported or indigenously produced.[13] Thus its safeguards are applicable in non–nuclear weapon states wherever nuclear material for peaceful purposes is found. By contrast, the INFCIRC/66 model safeguards agreement applies only to transferred nuclear items, items derived from them, and any other items that the state may place under safeguards; it does not affect other nuclear facilities in the importing nation.

From a nonproliferation standpoint, INFCIRC/66's item-only safeguards pose a particular problem: they cannot prevent replication of safeguarded technology or know-how for use in another, nonsafeguarded facility. India, for example, was able to produce a nuclear explosive device by copying technology from its safeguarded nuclear facilities, and Brazil transferred scientists from safeguarded nuclear facilities to its unsafeguarded (and now abandoned) "parallel" nuclear program for development of nuclear weapons. (Nuclear *material,* however, transferred from a safeguarded facility to a previously unsafeguarded one remains under safeguards. See the discussion of "pursuit" below.)

Euratom safeguards apply to all nuclear material for peaceful purposes in the member-states of the European Community. This makes them doubly comprehensive: they are full-scope safeguards, covering both imported and indigenously produced materials, and they cover these materials in all forms, including ores. The exception to the comprehensive scope of these safeguards is nuclear material used in the military programs of France and the United Kingdom. These nations exercised their option to end safeguards over the material by declaring it to be destined for military use.

A final safeguards concept, known as "pursuit," requires explanation for a complete understanding of the scope of safeguards. Pursuit simply means that safeguards are highly "contagious," often "contaminating" nuclear materials and facilities that are not included in a formal safeguards agreement. For example, nuclear material processed or derived from safeguarded material is also subject to safeguards. Thus, plutonium exiting a nuclear reactor is safeguarded if the uranium that produced it was safeguarded. Pursuit also means that safeguarded material introduced into an unsafeguarded nuclear plant "infects" the rest of the plant, bringing all material in the entire plant under safeguards. Safeguards on such a plant end only when all nuclear material is taken out of it.[14]

• Items Subject to Safeguards

INFCIRC/153 requires that signatories accept safeguards on all "source or special fissionable material." This refers to fissionable materials (Pu-239, U-233, and enriched uranium) that can be used, directly or after further processing, in a nuclear explosive. It also includes thorium.[15] It does not include uranium ore and yellowcake (the infant stages of the uranium lifecycle), although the transfer of yellowcake must be reported to the agency. INFCIRC/66 safeguards extend beyond special fissionable material to include the technology and facilities that produce this material. Like INFCIRC/153, it does not cover uranium ore, but it does cover yellowcake.

The emphasis on *nuclear material* in the more comprehensive document and on *nuclear facilities* in the older agreement has important implications for proliferation. The INFCIRC/153 agreement follows the flow of nuclear material through a facility and between facilities. Thus, material safeguarded under an INFCIRC/153–type agreement remains under safeguards even if transferred to a facility not originally listed in the agreement. On the other hand, INFCIRC/153 gives inspectors very limited access to nuclear facilities that do not contain nuclear materials.

By contrast, the nuclear facilities focus of INFCIRC/66–type agreements gives inspectors access to a safeguarded facility whether fissile material is present or not. Its weakness is that the IAEA would have no jurisdiction to safeguard material in a facility that is not covered by an INFCIRC/66 agreement (assuming that an INFCIRC/153 agreement does not also apply to the nation in question). The exception to this assertion concerns material transferred out of a facility under INFCIRC/66 safeguards. In such a case, safeguards would follow the material, even if it were transferred to a facility not originally covered by INFCIRC/66. Table 6.1 compares the INFCIRC/66 and INFCIRC/153 agreements.

HOW IS SAFEGUARDING CARRIED OUT?

A safeguards agreement such as INFCIRC/153 is actually composed of three documents, which detail the safeguards procedure. The broadest agreement, modeled on INFCIRC/153, outlines the obligations of the state and IAEA. A "subsidiary arrangement" lists the facilities to be safeguarded, and the "facility attachment" details the precise location of safeguards measurement points and camera placements in each facility, the areas to which inspectors will be allowed access, and the estimated frequency of inspections.

Sensitivity to questions of national sovereignty affects the choice of safeguarding tools available to the IAEA. Intrusive measures such as satellite reconnaissance, permanent in-house inspectors at all nuclear facilities, and international management or ownership of sensitive nuclear facilities are politically unfeasible. Instead, the IAEA relies heavily on more discreet means of verifying the nondiversion of fissile material. The system consists of three major components: materials accountancy, containment and surveillance, and inspections.[16]

Materials accountancy involves monitoring the flow of fissile materials into and out of a nuclear facility and between strategic points within the facility. These records are kept by the facility operator, and copies are forwarded regularly to the IAEA. IAEA inspectors use the records to account for fissile materials when carrying out their inspections.

The containment and surveillance element of the safeguards system includes a set of seals, cameras, sensors, and real-time alarm systems used to ensure that fissile materials have not been diverted since their last inspection.

Inspections are the most intrusive element of the safeguards system, but are kept to the minimum needed to fulfill the agency's mission. Inspections are routinely carried out only on declared nuclear facilities, and only at regular intervals. Provision is made for unannounced inspections of gas centrifuge facilities, but these can take place only in states that do not require a visa for entry (otherwise the visa application process "telegraphs" the arrival of an inspector).

SAFEGUARDING AUTHORITY OF THE IAEA AND EURATOM

IAEA and Euratom safeguarding prerogatives differ in two ways. First, Euratom has greater enforcement authority than the IAEA. Euratom is empowered to impose sanctions on persons or facilities, and can arraign a member-state before the European Court.[17] Beyond internal disciplinary action, the IAEA is limited to formally notifying the UN Security Council that the agency cannot verify the absence of diversion of nuclear material.

Second, Euratom safeguards begin earlier in the nuclear fuel cycle than those of the IAEA. Euratom safeguards are placed on uranium ore, whereas IAEA safeguards apply only once uranium is processed (the yellowcake stage), when import or export of the material must be reported to the agency. When the yellowcake is enriched or fabricated into fuel, full IAEA safeguards apply.[18]

Euratom and IAEA safeguarding jurisdictions overlap in the case of Euratom NNWS, all of whom are parties to the NPT. Negotiations on an acceptable division of labor between the two agencies were concluded in 1973. Under the interagency agreement, Euratom accepted primary responsibility for collecting and verifying accounting reports, which were then to be forwarded to the IAEA in Vienna.[19] Routine inspections would be handled by both agencies, but the IAEA inspections would be less frequent than those of Euratom. The two agencies would jointly inspect facilities containing highly enriched uranium or plutonium.[20]

In April 1992 Euratom and the IAEA agreed to revise these responsibilities on the basis of a "partnership" arrangement, which would cut costs by reducing redundancy in their safeguarding work.[21]

LIMITS ON IAEA SAFEGUARDS

International nuclear safeguards are relatively comprehensive, particularly given the political sensitivities of the various nations involved in negotiating them. Nevertheless, they are frequently criticized for a variety of shortcomings.

First, NPT-based inspections have in practice been limited to nuclear material declared by an NPT signatory. The list of facilities containing fissile material supplied by the NPT signatory is required to be comprehensive, but the agency cannot guarantee that this is the case. Obviously, the agency cannot inspect materials if it does not know they exist.[22]

Another shortcoming is more perceived than real. It is commonly believed that the IAEA cannot inspect a nuclear facility until nuclear material enters it. This belief is based on INFCIRC/153's designation of materials, rather than facilities, as the focus of inspection, and is a handicap only to the extent that the agency behaves as if it were true. Some analysts point out that INFCIRC/153 does make provision for inspection of facilities prior to the introduction of fissile material, and that the agreement places no limitations on the frequency or timing of these inspections.[23]

A third weakness in the safeguards system concerns the construction of nuclear facilities. Design information for nuclear facilities is normally provided to the IAEA too late for the agency to influence its construction in a way that would make the facility "safeguards friendly." However, in February 1992 the IAEA board of governors called on nations with full-scope safeguards to provide preliminary design information as soon as they decided to construct a new nuclear plant or modify an existing one. The board further requested that full design information be submitted at least six months prior to the start of construction. The European Community, Japan, and Canada are supportive of the idea, but how other nations will respond is unclear.

Fourth, the effectiveness of IAEA safeguards is also limited by the agency's skewed allocation of safeguards resources. More than 70 percent of the agency's safeguards budget is spent in Europe, Canada, and Japan, areas with large quantities of nuclear material but of little or no proliferation concern. Canadian nuclear facilities receive several hundred inspector-days of scrutiny per year, whereas only two visits annually were scheduled for Iraq's nuclear facilities prior to the Gulf War. This pattern of safeguarding results from an agency policy not to discriminate against any member-state in the administration of its programs. The result, however, is a relatively inefficient use of safeguards resources.

Fifth, the IAEA secretariat has traditionally been reluctant to use its power to conduct "special inspections" of a nation's nuclear facilities. These inspections—specifically provided for in the Treaty of Tlatelolco—are obliquely referred to in the NPT's model safeguards document, INFCIRC/153.[24] According to this document, the special inspections power allows the agency, after consulting with the state, to inspect locations not listed on the agency's routine inspections list for that country. The IAEA secretariat has never employed this power (its wide-ranging inspections in Iraq were carried out as part of a UN mandate), although the agency's board of governors reaffirmed in February 1992 the agency's right to conduct such inspections.

Finally, since 1986 IAEA safeguards have been weakened by the zero-growth budget policy adopted by the agency. The new policy, advocated by the United States and other nations concerned about the distended bureaucracies of some UN agencies, is a blow to effective safeguarding because it freezes the IAEA budget even as the number of facilities requiring inspections is increasing. In 1985, each safeguards dollar covered 556 significant quantities of nuclear material, whereas the same dollar was expected to cover 970 significant quantities in 1990.[25] As resources continue to be spread thinly, the possibilities for evasion of safeguards increases.

Considering the limitations on the IAEA's safeguards authority, the agency's record of safeguards work can arguably be regarded as exemplary. The extent to which the agency can strengthen its safeguarding work will depend in large measure on the support given it by its member-states.

NOTES

1. David Fischer notes that only a handful of states not party to the NPT or the Treaty of Tlatelolco still use INFCIRC/66. Argentina and Brazil are in the process of switching to a safeguards agreement based on the IAEA's more comprehensive INFCIRC/153 accord. The more comprehensive agreement would also replace INFCIRC/66 for Chile and Cuba, if these nations subscribe to the Tlatelolco treaty as expected. The same will occur in Algeria when that nation signs the NPT. These changes would leave only three states—India, Israel, and Pakistan—with INFCIRC/66 safeguards.

2. David Fischer and Paul Szasz, *Safeguarding the Atom: A Critical Appraisal* (Stockholm: International Peace Research Institute, 1985), p. 24.

3. D. Fischer, personal correspondence, July 9, 1992, p. 5.

4. Peter Kelly, *Safeguards in Europe* (Vienna: International Atomic Energy Agency, 1985), p. 28.

5. Ibid., p. 42.

6. Lawrence Scheinman, *The International Atomic Energy Agency and World Nuclear Order* (Washington, D.C.: Resources for the Future, 1987), p. 124.

7. Ibid., p. 123.

8. William C. Potter, *Nuclear Power and Nonproliferation: An Interdisciplinary Perspective* (Cambridge, Mass.: Oelgeschlager, Gunn & Hain, Publishers, 1982), p. 210.

9. INFCIRC/153, Article 28.

10. Scheinman, p. 165.

11. With time, experience, and testing, a state would learn to make a nuclear explosive with much less material. (D. Fischer, personal correspondence, July 9, 1992, p. 6.)

12. D. Fischer, personal correspondence, July 9, 1992, p. 6.

13. If the IAEA concludes, either from intelligence tips or from its own accounting information, that undeclared materials exist, it must try to ferret out such material and subject it to safeguards. (D. Fischer, personal correspondence, July 9, 1992, p. 6.)

14. D. Fischer, personal correspondence, July 9, 1992, p. 7.

15. International Atomic Energy Agency, *IAEA Safeguards Glossary, 1987 Edition* (Vienna: IAEA Division of Public Information, 1987), p. 10.

16. International Atomic Energy Agency, *International Safeguards and the Peaceful Uses of Nuclear Energy* (Vienna: IAEA Division of Public Information, n.d.), p. 1.

17. Kelly, p. 28.

18. Ibid., p. 29.

19. John Redick, "Argentina and Brazil's New Arrangement for Mutual Inspections and IAEA Safeguards," (Washington, D.C.: Nuclear Control Institute, February 1992), p. 3.

20. Ibid.

21. D. Fischer, personal correspondence, July 9, 1992, p. 8.

22. Recall, however, that the IAEA safeguarding mandate covers *all* nuclear material in a nation, not just declared material. If the IAEA has reason to believe that a state has undeclared nuclear material, it has the right and duty to seek out and safeguard such material.

23. Myron Kratzer, "How Can International Non-Proliferation Safeguards Be Made More Relevant?" (Washington, D.C.: The Atlantic Council, August 1991).

24. See INFCIRC/153, paragraph 73(b) and paragraph 77.

25. Mark Hibbs, "Gulf War Will Shift IAEA Safeguards Priorities—By How Much?" *Nucleonics Week* (February 20, 1992), p. 13.

7

The Politics of Proliferation

A variety of political considerations lies behind the decision to pursue a nuclear weapons capability. This chapter reviews the incentives and disincentives for seeking nuclear weapons, as well as the options available for dealing with their proliferation.[1]

IS THE SPREAD OF NUCLEAR WEAPONS INEVITABLE?

Nuclear proliferation is popularly regarded as unavoidable. The logic behind this belief appears to be sound: as the scientific and technological base of non–nuclear weapon states expands, the skills and technology needed to construct a nuclear force are likely to grow as well. No system of export controls, safeguards, or sanctions will permanently contain the spread of nuclear knowledge. President Kennedy's often-cited 1963 prediction that ten nations could possess a nuclear bomb by 1970, and fifteen to twenty by 1975, was based on this line of reasoning.

Happily, the historical record does not support such pessimism: only six nations had detonated a nuclear explosive by 1975. Although nations do tend to advance scientifically and technologically (but even this is not guaranteed), it is a mistake to assume that having the ability to build a bomb automatically leads to a decision to do so. The list of nations judged capable of joining the nuclear club, but which have not, is long indeed. The point is further reinforced by recalling that several nations began nuclear weapons programs but later terminated them: Sweden, Brazil, South Africa, and probably South Korea and Taiwan.

The noninevitability of nuclear proliferation has important consequences for nonproliferation policy. Some observers argue that policymakers can think in terms of *winning* the nonproliferation battle rather than simply *managing* it.[2] Winning here means more than persuading would-be nuclear nations to forgo pursuit of the bomb. It also implies the possibility of persuading even de facto nuclear weapon states such as Israel, India, and Pakistan to end their military nuclear programs and eventually to divest themselves of nuclear weapons. By contrast, nonproliferation policy based on managing the spread of nuclear weapons often assumes that significant reversals of nuclear programs are not possible, and that nations with nuclear weapons are at best likely to agree to cap the expansion in their arsenal rather than eliminate their stocks completely.

Whatever strategy a nation uses in its nonproliferation policy, an understanding of the incentives and disincentives for pursuit of a nuclear capability is necessary. These factors are examined below.

INCENTIVES FOR DEVELOPING NUCLEAR WEAPONS

Nations seek nuclear weapons for a variety of reasons, but one motivation—security—stands clearly above all others. A nuclear weapon may appear to be the ultimate guarantor of a nation's security for several reasons. First, it can be used as a deterrent, forcing opponents to think long and hard about the consequences of aggression against a nuclear-armed state. Alternatively, a nuclear weapon could be used as a psychological tool to intimidate or blackmail a targeted government. Finally, a nuclear weapon could be employed in battle as a massive show of force designed to persuade an opponent to desist.

Still, most nations interested in acquiring a nuclear capability for security reasons have done so only after being faced with what Thomas Graham calls an *acute* security threat, frequently the threat of nuclear force against it. As examples, he cites the U.S. nuclear threat against China, the former Soviet threat against Israel, the Chinese threat against India, and the Indian threat against Pakistan. Each threatened state faced acute security dangers that influenced the decision to develop nuclear weapons.

A second reason cited for the pursuit of a nuclear weapons capability is enhanced prestige. Many nations equate nuclear capability with greater respect in the international community; nuclear power frequently brings a nation greater status in international fora and offers increased autonomy for many nations. The United Kingdom and France, for example, are both known to have sought nuclear weapons as much for the perceived prestige associated with the new technology as for the security they expected to derive from it.[3]

A third factor that can push a nation to seek nuclear weapons has been partially addressed: technological momentum. Although a high level of technological development does not automatically lead to the pursuit of nuclear weapons, it can be an impetus to move in this direction. This was especially true in the first two decades after the dawn of the nuclear age, when the norm against the development of nuclear weapons was not as strong as it is today. The nuclear programs of the United Kingdom and France were both driven in part by technological momentum.

Finally, domestic factors may influence the decision to develop a nuclear weapon. Strong public support for the bomb or bureaucratic pressures to build one may impel the political leadership to move in that direction. France's program, for example, was driven in part by bureaucratic inertia: the Ministry of Defense and the Commissariat a l'Energie Atomique collaborated on a nuclear weapons program for at least seventeen months before official cabinet-level approval of the activity in April 1958.[4]

DISINCENTIVES FOR DEVELOPING NUCLEAR WEAPONS

The calculus behind the decision to "go nuclear" is more complex than it may first appear. Despite the appeal of becoming a nuclear power, nations are persuaded more often than not to forgo pursuit of a nuclear weapon. The factors leading a nation away from development of nuclear weapons are discussed below.

First, certain security considerations argue more strongly against acquisition of the weapon than for it. A nation crossing the nuclear threshold has won a great psychological victory, but possession of a single device is likely to jeopardize its security by making it a tempting target for preemptive attack. Even if a country has several weapons, they may not serve as a credible deterrent if they are perceived to be vulnerable to attack; an enemy may believe it more prudent to launch a preemptive strike than to allow a modest nuclear arsenal to grow. Thus a nation serious about incorporating a nuclear component into its military strategy must consider the development not only of nuclear weapons, but also of means for protecting them from attack.

Consideration must also be given to the question of a delivery system for the weapon. Missiles are often the preferred means of getting a nuclear bomb to its target because they are more likely to deliver a bomb accurately than aircraft or other delivery systems. All the nations of current proliferation concern either possess ballistic missiles or are developing them, but technical hurdles, such as miniaturizing nuclear warheads for use on a missile, are still faced by most of these nations.[5] Other means of delivery, such as aircraft or even truck or ship, are less reliable and/or offer fewer targeting options.

Another headache for nuclear aspirants is the security of nuclear weapon stocks. Many aspiring nuclear weapon states have unstable governments, and the possibility of weapons falling into the hands of rival domestic groups or terrorists cannot be discounted. This possibility increases if the weapons are made mobile, as a government might wish them to be in order to avoid attack from enemies outside the nation's borders.

A second disincentive to nuclear weapons development is the increasing delegitimization of nuclear weapons. Today the development of nuclear weapons is more likely to evoke international condemnation than admiration. Evidence of the increasing strength of this norm is the manner in which France and India became nuclear powers. France announced its pursuit of the bomb and proclaimed itself a nuclear power following its successful test. Fourteen years later, India was compelled to carry out its test secretly and to label it a peaceful nuclear explosion.[6] With the end of the Cold War and the sweeping U.S.-Russian arms reduction accords, the delegitimization of nuclear explosives has been carried still further.

Third, nations may also be dissuaded from embarking on a nuclear weapons program because of high costs. Although a variety of reports in the 1960s and 1970s documented the declining cost of manufacturing a nuclear weapon (from $2 billion for the Manhattan Project to an estimated $51 million in 1976),[7] these reports appear not to have included the cost of sensitive facilities such as enrichment or reprocessing plants, which are necessary if a nation expects to maintain fissile material production for weapons use. Because export controls have made the purchase of sensitive nuclear facilities extremely difficult, most would-be proliferants must now assemble their own facilities component by component, with items made indigenously or imported on the black market. This inefficient process is quite costly: Iraq is estimated to have spent billions of dollars in its unsuccessful quest for the bomb. For nations facing a variety of urgent development issues requiring large-scale investment, the costs of a nuclear weapons development program may be prohibitive.

Fourth, just as the real cost of developing nuclear weapons is probably greater than previously believed, the technical difficulties involved may be tougher to surmount than expected. Nations seeking to enter the nuclear arena still require long lead times—typically a decade or more—to advance from the decision to pursue a bomb to its completion.[8] The technical precision required for enrichment, reprocessing, and weapons fabrication demands advanced technology. The spheres of fissile material used in a nuclear weapon, for example, must be perfectly round; the slightest imperfection could cause the weapons to fissile. Such precision is usually far beyond the capability of most nations.

A fifth disincentive to the development of a nuclear weapons capability is the possibility of international sanctions against transgressor nations. Although such measures are difficult to organize effectively, they may be more attractive after exposure of Iraq's massive and secret nuclear effort.

OPTIONS FOR NONPROLIFERATION POLICY

The post–Cold War, post–Gulf War international environment is ripe for a multipronged strategy for controlling, if not winning, the battle against nuclear proliferation. Initiatives in this area can be divided into supply-side solutions, which deal with the control of materials and technologies that can contribute to a nuclear capability, and demand-side solutions, which address the factors that impel a nation to pursue a nuclear weapons capability.

• Supply-side Options

In general, the supply side of the proliferation problem has been given the greatest attention by the regime and shows the greatest number of successes. However, most regime structures controlling the supply of nuclear materials and technology could use strengthening.

Safeguards. International safeguards hold a nation accountable for the disposition of its stock of nuclear materials and provide disincentives to anything but the peaceful use of these materials. Safeguards cover most nuclear facilities around the world, but those that remain uncovered are of great concern. Weaknesses in the safeguards system, including inadequate access to suspect facilities and to facilities under construction, are discussed in Chapter 6. Recall that current international safeguards are designed to alert the international community of possible diversion of nuclear materials, not to prevent such diversion. They must be used in conjunction with other supply-side measures to ensure reasonably effective control of nuclear materials.

Export controls. Export controls are an excellent complement to safeguards for regulating the flow and use of nuclear materials. The controls of the Zangger Committee and the Nuclear Suppliers Group (described briefly in Chapter 5) have made the acquisition of nuclear materials and technology without safeguards more difficult. The April 1992 extension of the Nuclear Suppliers Group "trigger list" to cover dual-use items will strengthen the controls significantly. Today, the acquisition of sensitive nuclear facilities such as a reprocessing or enrichment plant, even with safeguards, is almost unheard of.

Bilateral controls also help regulate the flow of nuclear materials and may be stricter than the multilateral controls of the Nuclear Suppliers Group. U.S. export controls were significantly stricter than those of the NSG in requiring full-scope safeguards as a condition of export and in prohibiting the transfer of U.S.-supplied nuclear materials or technology to third parties without U.S. consent. Today the NSG has adopted these policies as well. The Soviet Union until recently required the return of spent fuel from reactors it supplied overseas, making it unavailable for nonpeaceful uses in the importing nation.[9] This was a very effective bilateral export control measure that has not been emulated by multilateral export control groups such as the NSG.

Some argue that export controls are counterproductive in the long run. They may serve to isolate and alienate a state from the regime, and they may encourage the state to embark on its own indigenous path of sensitive technology development. This course of events appears to have been followed in India, Brazil, and Iraq. The increasing international affirmation of the norm of nonproliferation, however, is likely to help retard indigenous development of nuclear facilities in all but a handful of states.

Extension of the NPT. Both safeguards and export controls have significant roots in the NPT, and successful extension of the treaty in 1995 would constitute a strong boost to supply-side regime controls. (The NPT also supports the demand side of the proliferation equation by building confidence in the peaceful character of nuclear programs around the world, thereby reducing the incentive to build a nuclear explosive capability.)

• Demand-side Options

Management strategies that address the demand for nuclear explosives seek to reduce the incentives for acquiring nuclear weapons and are of increasing interest in the regime. Most of the options mentioned below can be used whether the goal is to prevent proliferation from starting, or to cap or even roll back an existing nuclear program.

Security guarantees. Nations that seek nuclear weapons for security reasons may be dissuaded from pursuing this technology if measures are taken to enhance their security. One such initiative was taken in 1968 when the three depositary states for the NPT (the United Kingdom, the United States, and the USSR) each pledged to seek UN Security Council assistance for any NPT non–nuclear weapon state that was the target of nuclear aggression or was threatened by such aggression. Reaffirmation of Resolution 255 could give a nation the confidence it needs to develop its security policy without resorting to the nuclear option.[10]

Another security measure, the "negative security guarantee," calls for restraint, rather than action, by nuclear weapon states. Under the policy, nuclear weapon states pledge not to use nuclear weapons against a non–nuclear weapon state. The five officially recognized nuclear weapon states have each issued their own versions of such assurances. The United States, for example, reserves the right to use nuclear weapons against a non–nuclear weapon state that is allied to a nuclear weapon state. Other nations offer more comprehensive guarantees.

Some argue that the desire for nuclear weapons can be preempted through the provision of conventional arms to the potential proliferant. This solution may be less than ideal, as it could lead to a destabilizing conventional arms race and may not in fact achieve the goal of averting nuclear weapons development. In addition, nations could conceivably use the threat of development of nuclear weapons as a means to obtain conventional arms that otherwise are unavailable to them. Arming a nation with an array of conventional arms is preferable to having it develop nuclear weapons, but more creative solutions are available to dissuade a nation from taking the nuclear plunge.

Arms control measures. Several regional or international arms control measures can also help stem the spread of nuclear weapons. Nations unprepared to commit to unilateral nuclear disarmament may be more willing to abide by the terms of a nuclear weapon–free zone (NWFZ) in their region, under which nations in a particular geographical area pledge not to allow the possession, production, testing, or stationing of nuclear weapons in the region. NWFZs have been established in Antarctica and the South Pacific, and the Treaty of Tlatelolco will establish an important NWFZ in Latin America if Argentina, Brazil, Chile, and Cuba follow the rest of Latin America in adhering to the treaty, as expected. NWFZs have been proposed for South Asia, the Middle East, and other unstable regions, and are an effective means of stopping the spread of nuclear weapons before it starts.

Another arms control measure of great interest in the regime is the completion of a Comprehensive Test Ban (CTB) Treaty. This proposed treaty would extend the conditions of the Limited Test Ban Treaty to prohibit *all* nuclear tests. Many non–nuclear weapon states view the CTB as the litmus test of the nuclear weapon states' commitment to disarmament and to fulfillment of their obligations under Article VI of the NPT. Russia and France both stopped testing voluntarily in 1991–1992, and have declared their willingness to extend the temporary ban if all nuclear powers join them.

The United States and the United Kingdom have long been reluctant to commit to a CTB, although this position may be changing. The U.S. Congress responded to the Russian moratorium on testing with a nine-month moratorium in 1992 that requires the president to submit legislation for a CTB to Congress by 1996. The U.S. moratorium was later extended through September 1994, and Russia responded in kind. The United Kingdom, whose nuclear tests are carried out at the U.S. test site in Nevada, is obliged to honor U.S. policy on nuclear testing. The Russian, French, and U.S. initiatives, coupled with continuing pressure on nuclear weapon states to make progress on disarmament issues before the 1995 NPT extension conference, could create the international political climate necessary for conclusion of a CTB.

Punitive measures. Economic sanctions and military force are other options available to reduce demand for a nuclear weapons program.

Whether economic sanctions are successful in dissuading a nation from pursuing a nuclear weapons program depends on the extent of the sanctions and the stage of development of the nuclear program at the time sanctions are introduced. Military force may be effective in eliminating a nuclear program (although it was not in Iraq), but the political costs associated with this option can be extensive.

NOTES

1. Except where noted, this section draws from Chapters 5 and 6 of William C. Potter, *Nuclear Power and Nonproliferation: An Interdisciplinary Perspective* (Cambridge, Mass.: Oelgeschlager, Gunn & Hain, Publishers, 1982). See that volume for a more detailed discussion of the issues treated below.

2. See Thomas W. Graham, "Winning the Nonproliferation Battle," *Arms Control Today* (September 1991).

3. Lewis Dunn, *Controlling the Bomb: Nuclear Proliferation in the 1980's* (New Haven, Conn.: Yale University Press, 1982), p. 8.

4. Ibid., p. 9.

5. Lewis Dunn, "Containing Nuclear Proliferation," *Adelphi Papers* (Winter 1991), p. 18.

6. Dunn, *Controlling the Bomb,* p. 17.

7. See Mitchell Reiss, *Without the Bomb: The Politics of Nuclear Nonproliferation* (New York: Columbia University Press, 1988), p. 28. This is the cost of designing, building, and testing a plutonium-based nuclear device. Reiss notes that if a nation already possessed its own fissile material, the 1976 cost would fall still further, to around $1 million.

8. Thomas W. Graham, "Winning the Nonproliferation Battle," *Arms Control Today* (September 1991), p. 10.

9. For environmental reasons, Russia apparently no longer maintains this requirement.

10. Dunn, "Containing Nuclear Proliferation," p. 43.

8

The 1995 NPT Extension Conference

The fate of the Nuclear Non-Proliferation Treaty will be determined at a historic conference of treaty parties in New York in spring 1995. Many misconceptions surround the meeting, however. This chapter explores the issues and significance of the 1995 gathering.

PURPOSE AND SIGNIFICANCE OF THE CONFERENCE

Unlike the treaties of Tlatelolco and Rarotonga, the NPT is not "of a permanent nature"; it does not continue in force indefinitely. Instead, Article X.2 calls for a conference twenty-five years after the treaty's entry into force to determine the length of its extension. Significantly, the article does not offer conference delegates the option to terminate the treaty directly, although termination could result from action taken at the conference, as discussed below.

Treaty extension is the only NPT-mandated business on the conference agenda; however, other activity is likely to take place. Review conferences to assess the treaty's implementation have been held every five years since 1975, and will probably be held in 1995 as well. Complaints regarding perceived treaty deficiencies are aired at such review conferences, and in 1995 this could affect the vote on treaty extension. Review conferences are also used as fora for attempts to amend the treaty, which could complicate treaty extension prospects in 1995 as well. Concerns surrounding the NPT and problems associated with amending it are considered below.

OPTIONS SURROUNDING TREATY EXTENSION

Article X.2 clearly requires a decision on the length of the NPT's extension; however, several questions remain regarding the specifics of this requirement and the process for bringing it about.

• Length of the Extension

Treaty language regarding its extension has implications that are not read-ily apparent. As noted above, delegates are not given a direct option to ter-minate the treaty.[1] Instead, Article X.2 allows them three options:

1. Vote for the treaty to continue in force indefinitely.
2. Vote to extend the treaty for an additional period.
3. Vote to extend the treaty for additional periods.

The first option—to extend the treaty indefinitely—is clear. The third option likely requires extension of the treaty for an indefinite number of additional periods, at the end of each of which the parties could vote to terminate the treaty or to renew it for another period.[2]

The second option—to extend the treaty for a single additional pe-riod—has an enormous hidden implication. Extension of the treaty for an additional period would necessarily imply its termination at the end of that period. This is because the NPT provides for no mechanism to further ex-tend the treaty at the end of a single additional term. In this way, treaty parties could plant the seeds of the NPT's demise in 1995, even though Article X.2 does not offer termination as a direct option.

It is possible that treaty delegates could reach no conclusion regarding the treaty's extension, in which case its status would be unclear. Some ex-perts argue that in such a case the NPT would continue in force provision-ally, whereas others believe that no action at the end of the conference pe-riod would signal the treaty's termination.[3]

• Conditional Extension

Delegates may seek to make treaty extension dependent on the fulfillment of certain conditions such as progress in arms control, a contentious issue for some treaty parties. The NPT, however, makes no provision for condi-tional extension as such. To impose conditions would be to amend the NPT, and would require following procedures for amendment.[4] The con-ference could, however, adopt resolutions that reflect the views of the con-ference delegates on issues of concern, but resolutions would not be legally binding on treaty parties.

• Treaty Amendments

Conference delegates may view 1995, the year of treaty extension, as an appropriate time to pause and consider amendments to the NPT. The treaty makes provision for amendments, but the requirements for amendment are stiff. All NWS and all members of the IAEA's board of governors, in addition to a majority of NPT parties, must support such a change. The board of governors is a heterogeneous group of thirty-five nations with widely divergent views on nuclear issues, and the likelihood that all could be persuaded to support a significant treaty amendment is slim.

The effect on the 1995 extension conference of an attempt to amend the treaty process is uncertain. However, it is likely that failure to agree on an amendment would harm prospects for a lengthy treaty extension.

POTENTIAL CONFERENCE DIFFICULTIES

Many of the rules governing the 1995 conference, from procedural issues to the scope of the meeting agenda, have yet to be decided. A preparatory committee made up of interested NPT parties will address these issues. Some difficulties at the conference, however, can be anticipated.

• Conference Attendance

The language used in Article X.2 gives an important advantage to opponents of a lengthy treaty extension. It stipulates that the decision to extend the NPT "shall be taken by a majority of Parties to the Treaty" rather than by a majority of parties attending the conference. Absentee nations would in effect cast a "no" vote, and a minority of treaty parties in attendance at the extension conference could block lengthy (or any) extension of the treaty. This rule makes the issue of conference attendance an important one.

If attendance at past NPT review conferences is any guide, the absentee rate at the 1995 conference could be substantial and possibly pivotal. An average of 37 percent of treaty signatories missed the four review conferences held between 1975 and 1990.[5] A similar absentee rate in 1995 would automatically give opponents of an extension resolution fifty-seven "no" votes (37 percent of an estimated NPT membership of 150 at the time of the conference), allowing extension opponents to prevail with only twenty additional "no" or "abstain" votes from conference attendees. The importance of the 1995 conference will probably encourage a higher attendance rate than that of past review conferences (in fact, 123 nations were represented at the first preparatory meeting for the extension conference, held in May 1993), but the implications of the language used in Article X.2 should not be underestimated.

• Fulfillment of Article VI

A group of NPT non–nuclear weapon states has complained since the first review conference in 1975 that the nuclear powers have not complied with Article VI, which requires them to pursue negotiations to end the nuclear arms race and to work toward nuclear disarmament. For the NNWS in question, the lack of movement toward these goals is tantamount to a breach of contract. Some observers fear that these nuclear have-not nations may require an NWS commitment to a Comprehensive Test Ban in 1995 as the quid pro quo for their support of a lengthy treaty extension.

The issue has long plagued the NPT review conferences. At the 1990 meeting, Mexico led a group of nations in blocking agreement on a final conference document (which required unanimous approval) because of U.S. and British refusals to commit to a Comprehensive Test Ban, which would outlaw all nuclear tests. The Mexican-led delegation numbered only nine nations, but given the rules for passage of treaty extension outlined above, this may be a significant base from which to lobby for greater NWS attention to disarmament measures.[6]

The nuclear test ban issue continues to be treated seriously by many NPT party states. At the 1991 Limited Test Ban Treaty Conference, called to explore the possibility of expanding the LTBT to a CTB, 100 of the 117 signatories to the LTBT attended. Most of these nations are also parties to the NPT. The overwhelming majority of the sixty nations making statements at the conference spoke in favor of a comprehensive test ban.[7] Rigid opposition to a CTB from the United States and Great Britain blocked consensus on the issue, but the conference voted seventy-five to two, with nineteen abstentions, to reconsider the issue at a reconvened conference, probably before the 1995 NPT extension conference.[8] Continued U.S. and British opposition to a CTB at a reconvened LTBT conference could sour the mood of delegates to the 1995 NPT meeting and jeopardize chances for a lengthy extension of the NPT.

Despite the problems created by the CTB issue, many observers are increasingly confident that a lengthy treaty extension will result from the 1995 meeting. This confidence can be attributed to the increased influence enjoyed by the United States in what is perceived as a unipolar world, the drastic reductions in nuclear arms by Russia and the United States, and the increasingly widely shared belief in the value of the NPT.

WHAT WOULD NONRENEWAL OF THE TREATY MEAN?

In the unlikely event that the 1995 NPT extension conference votes to extend the treaty for only a single term (after which it would expire), the implications for the nonproliferation regime would be significant. Withdrawal of support for the NPT would weaken global adherence to the norm of nonproliferation and would eliminate the most important international legal barrier to the pursuit of a nuclear weapons capability.

Termination of the NPT could have a devastating effect on the world's nuclear safeguards system. The model NPT safeguards agreement,

INFCIRC/153, remains in force for NPT signatories "as long as the State is a party" to the NPT. Termination of the treaty, therefore, would appear to release NPT parties from their NPT-mandated safeguards obligations. These safeguards obligations are of two types: (1) full-scope safeguards on fissile material (mandated for the 144 NPT NNWS by Article III.1 of the NPT) and (2) item-only safeguards (mandated for the nuclear exports of all 147 NPT parties by Article III.2). The lapse of these obligations is an eventuality of serious concern, but four factors mitigate its impact.

First, the demise of the NPT would not affect safeguards unrelated to the NPT. Safeguards required by the treaties of Tlatelolco and Rarotonga, as well as Euratom safeguards and some of the IAEA's INFCIRC/66 agreements, would all continue unimpeded.

Second, termination of the NPT would automatically reactivate pre-NPT tripartite agreements among the IAEA, the United States, and U.S. nuclear customers. These agreements, however, are generally more limited in scope than the full-scope NPT safeguards they would replace.[9]

Third, some international legal scholars argue that the end of the NPT would mean the end of safeguards obligations only on new transfers or development of fissile material. Material under safeguards at the time of the treaty's termination, they argue, would continue to be safeguarded, as would successive generations of nuclear material produced from the original, safeguarded stock.[10]

Finally, it is important to recall that nations subscribe voluntarily to safeguards, presumably because their interests are served by doing so. It is very possible that despite the treaty's termination, nations would find a method to maintain a safeguards system. New safeguards agreements could be negotiated, or more simply, pledges of continued adherence to existing safeguards agreements could be worked out.

NOTES

1. Actually, international law provides that treaties without a termination clause (such as the NPT) may be terminated at any time with the unanimous approval of the parties. The point here is that treaty termination was not intended by Article X.2 to be an option for the 1995 conference.

2. David Fischer, "Article X.2 of the Nuclear Non-Proliferation Treaty and the Nature of its 1995 Extension Conference," in George Bunn, Charles Van Doren, and David Fischer, *Options and Opportunities: The NPT Extension Conference of 1995* (Southampton: Programme for Promoting Nuclear Non-Proliferation, 1991), pp. 28–29. Fischer also considers the possibility of a limited number of additional fixed periods but finds this option logically untenable.

3. David Fischer argues the first scenario, but acknowledges other interpretations. See Bunn, Van Doren, and Fischer, pp. 31, 35–38.

4. George Bunn and Charles Van Doren, "Options for Extension of the NPT: The Intention of the Drafters of Article X.2," in Bunn, Van Doren, and Fischer, p. 12.

5. Calculated from data in David Fischer, *The International Nonproliferation Regime, 1987* (New York: United Nations, 1987), p. 28, and Bunn, Van Doren, and Fischer, p. 23.

6. William Epstein, "Conference a Qualified Success," *Bulletin of the Atomic Scientists* (December 1990), p. 46.

7. Tom Zamora, "LTBT Amendment Conference to Continue, but No Test Ban in Sight," *Arms Control Today* (March 1991), pp. 14–15.

8. Ibid., p. 16.

9. Charles Van Doren, "Safeguards and Technical Constraints in the 1990's," in John Simpson, ed., *Nuclear Nonproliferation: An Agenda for the 1990's*, Ford/Southampton Studies in North/South Security Relations (Cambridge: Cambridge University Press, 1987), p. 182.

10. Ibid., p. 180.

9

Nations of Proliferation Concern

As the nonproliferation regime has grown in strength, the number of nations of proliferation concern has dwindled. This chapter describes the attitudes and capabilities of nations currently or recently interested in developing nuclear weapons. The survey also covers China, whose history of imprudent nuclear exports merits attention.

NUCLEAR AND POTENTIAL NUCLEAR STATES

The following classification scheme gives a quick overview of the nuclear status of selected states.

- *Nuclear weapon states:* The United States, Russia, China, France, and the United Kingdom. Having manufactured and detonated a nuclear explosive prior to 1967, these states are officially designated "nuclear weapon states" by the NPT.
- *De facto nuclear weapon states:* India, Israel, Pakistan, and South Africa. This category covers a wide range of capabilities, from Israel, with warheads numbering in the hundreds, to Pakistan, which may not yet have a nuclear explosive but could assemble one at any time. These nations do not qualify as nuclear weapon states under the NPT definition.
- *Advanced threshold countries:* Argentina, Brazil, South Korea, and Taiwan. These nations have the technical capability to build nuclear weapons and once expressed interest in doing so, but have decided not to.
- *Potential threshold states:* Algeria, Iran, Iraq, Libya, and North Korea. These nations are still some distance from a nuclear capability, but are believed to be interested in pursuing such a capability.

The survey that follows examines states from the last three categories, with the exception of South Korea and Taiwan, whose interests in a nuclear weapons program appear to have ended in the 1970s, and Libya, whose efforts at acquiring nuclear arms have been sporadic and inconsistent. The survey includes a passage on the former Soviet Union, whose constituent republics present some unusual proliferation problems, and on China, whose export activities are of concern.

• Algeria

U.S. satellite photos of a Chinese-supplied nuclear reactor in the Algerian desert early in 1991 raised eyebrows in the U.S. intelligence community. Antiaircraft defenses surrounded the complex, and no power lines to carry electricity to the nation's cities were evident.[1] These characteristics, combined with the secret nature of the facility and the fact that Algeria is not a party to the NPT, prompted speculation that Algeria was in pursuit of material for nuclear weapons. The reactor appeared to be larger than Algeria claimed it was, which further raised suspicions. Experts estimate that the Algerian reactor could produce enough plutonium for a primitive bomb by 1995. However, Algeria signed a safeguards agreement for the reactor with the IAEA in February 1992, easing fears that the unit was intended for weapons material production.[2]

Involvement in nuclear commerce. In addition to its trade with China, Algeria's nuclear program has been assisted by Argentina, which has sold Algeria large amounts of uranium dioxide as well as a research reactor.

Attitude toward nonproliferation. Algeria announced in January 1992 its intention to sign the NPT, but did not say when it would do so. It is unclear how the change in Algerian regime since that time will affect Algerian plans.[3]

Unsafeguarded nuclear facilities. All nuclear facilities subject to safeguards in Algeria are safeguarded.

• Argentina and Brazil

The 1990–1991 nuclear policy turnabout in Argentina and Brazil reduced international concern over their nuclear programs. Still, the long history of interest in nuclear weapons in these South American nations warrants a review of each program. Because Argentine and Brazilian nuclear histories are so tightly intertwined, and because their policy shifts toward "nuclear transparency" have been a joint effort, these two Latin American nuclear giants are considered here together.

Argentina and Brazil began to acquire the infrastructure needed to produce nuclear weapons in the 1970s. Brazil signed the "deal of the century" with West Germany in 1975, under which Brazil was to purchase eight nuclear reactors as well as sensitive uranium enrichment and plutonium reprocessing plants. The facilities were sold under item-only safeguards, leaving open the possibility that the transferred technology, although safeguarded itself, could be copied to unsafeguarded facilities in Brazil's "parallel" nuclear program. Argentina, meanwhile, began construction in 1978 of its own sensitive facilities: a commercial-scale reprocessing plant at Ezeiza and a secret uranium enrichment plant at Pilcaniyeu. Disclosure of the Pilcaniyeu plant in 1983 reportedly persuaded Brazilian officials of the need for a Brazilian nuclear weapons program.[4]

By the mid-1980s, however, civilian governments and sour economic conditions prompted new thinking on nuclear policy in both nations. In 1985, Argentine president Raul Alfonsin and Brazilian president Jose Sarney held the first in a series of summit meetings over several years aimed at building confidence in the peaceful character of each nation's nuclear program. These meetings resulted in reciprocal inspections—sometimes carried out by the presidents themselves—of sensitive nuclear facilities in each nation.

Successors of the two men, Carlos Menem of Argentina and Fernando Collor of Brazil, continued the reciprocal visits and moved further away from their nuclear weapons programs. The policy of nuclear transparency declared by Collor led to the 1990 admission by Brazil that it had indeed sponsored a nuclear weapons program. Collor took a personal role in dismantling the program when he traveled to the Amazon jungle in September and wielded a shovel to help close a nuclear test site. Two months later, he met with Menem to sign a declaration forswearing the development of nuclear weapons and pledging regular inspections of Brazilian and Argentine nuclear facilities. This agreement was formalized in a July 1991 document called the Accord for the Exclusively Peaceful Use of Nuclear Energy, which established the Argentine-Brazilian Agency for Accounting and Control, a regional safeguarding agency similar to Euratom in Europe. Like Euratom, ABACC works closely with the IAEA in fulfilling its safeguards mission.

Involvement in nuclear commerce. Argentina and Brazil both regard nuclear exports as a valuable source of much needed hard currency. The two nations provide nuclear services to each other and are negotiating to sell uranium jointly to Germany. Argentina also has nuclear ventures planned or under way with Turkey and with other Latin American nations.

Attitude toward nonproliferation. Argentina and Brazil regard the NPT as unjustifiably discriminatory and have refused to subscribe to it.

However, the two nations are close to bringing into force the Treaty of Tlatelolco, and their recent safeguards agreements demonstrate a serious commitment to the nonproliferation regime. In addition, Argentina has agreed to abide by the export rules of the Nuclear Suppliers Group[5] and has been accepted for membership in the Missile Technology Control Regime.[6]

Unsafeguarded nuclear facilities. The safeguards agreements signed with ABACC and the IAEA are full-scope, leaving no unsafeguarded nuclear facilities in either nation.

• China

Official Chinese nuclear policy was increasingly supportive of the nonproliferation regime in the 1980s, but the export behavior of some Chinese ministries has led many to question the nation's commitment to halting the spread of nuclear weapons. Although China joined the International Atomic Energy Agency in 1984 and promised to require full-scope safeguards on its nuclear exports, nonproliferation policy in the 1980s appeared to take a back seat to the effort by individual ministries to earn hard currency for their own survival.

Involvement in nuclear commerce. Dangerous Chinese nuclear sales in the 1980s included the supply of enriched uranium to Brazil, heavy water to India and Argentina, and, perhaps of greatest concern, tritium, highly enriched uranium, and the design for a nuclear weapon to Pakistan. China continued to market its nuclear wares into the 1990s, offering research reactors to Algeria and a power reactor to Pakistan and signing a contract for the construction of four power reactors and a research center in Iran.[7] The sale of nuclear reactors to Egypt and Bangladesh and of a micro nuclear reactor to Ghana were also under discussion in 1992.[8]

Attitude toward nonproliferation. China's accession to the NPT is welcomed by most nations as an asset to the regime, but China's position as a nuclear supplier is still open to criticism. China has not indicated if it would require full-scope safeguards as a condition of export or if it would follow other supplier restrictions as called for by the Nuclear Suppliers Group. Its continuing negotiations with Pakistan—which has not accepted full-scope safeguards—over the sale of a nuclear reactor at Chashma appear to indicate that China will tolerate few restrictions on its right to supply nuclear goods to other nations.

Unsafeguarded nuclear facilities. As an NPT nuclear weapon state, China is not required to safeguard its nuclear facilities or material.

• Former Soviet Union

The dissolution of the Soviet Union in 1991 created new and unforeseen proliferation problems. Four nations—Belarus, Kazakhstan, Russia, and Ukraine—were left with Soviet strategic nuclear weapons on their territories, and a host of other republics were in possession of tactical nuclear devices. Instability in these territories and inexperience with export controls in the non-Russian republics led observers to fear a hemorrhage of nuclear materials, equipment, and know-how from these republics to nations coveting nuclear weapons. Although significant differences in nuclear assets, attitudes toward nonproliferation, and involvement in nuclear commerce can be found across the fifteen republics of the former Soviet Union, the interdependence of policies in the various republics justifies group treatment of proliferation issues in the region.

Involvement in nuclear commerce. Few of the many reports of nuclear leakage from the former Soviet Union in 1991 and 1992 have been substantiated, and none has involved significant quantities of weapons-related nuclear materials.[9] No evidence has surfaced of Kazakhstan's alleged sale of two tactical nuclear weapons to Iran,[10] nor of the transfer of a third to another country in the Middle East.[11] The much feared "brain drain" of nuclear scientists and technicians has not materialized, although attempts at emigration have been cited.[12] In short, the borders of former Soviet republics appear to be less porous than anticipated at the time of the breakup of the Soviet Union.

This upbeat assessment, however, applies only to materials and technology used primarily in the nuclear realm. The picture is much less sanguine with regard to exports of dual-use products, those apparently innocuous items that might also be used to advance a nuclear weapons capability.[13] Ukrainian and Estonian involvement in dual-use exports are of particular concern. Ukraine has exported tons of zirconium and hafnium —both restricted under Nuclear Suppliers Group guidelines—to Europe for reshipment to unknown countries. Estonia has emerged as a major transshipment point for Russian zirconium bound for unknown destinations.[14]

Attitude toward nonproliferation. Russia is recognized as the continuator state of the former Soviet Union; as such it has inherited the USSR's NPT status as a nuclear weapon state. Belarus, Kazakhstan, and Ukraine completed the transfer to Russia of tactical nuclear weapons on their soil and are expected to surrender the strategic nuclear weapons based on their territory by the end of the decade. The three nations stated in May 1992 that they will join the NPT as nonnuclear states, but only Belarus has made significant progress to this end, its parliament having voted to accede to the NPT in February 1993. Kazakhstan, although not having signed the NPT, requested admission to the IAEA in January 1993, as well as the initiation of safeguards negotiations.[15]

Ukraine has been the slowest of the former Soviet republics to embrace a clear nonproliferation stance. After renouncing nuclear weapons on achieving independence in 1991, Ukraine in 1993 was hedging on its commitment to ratify the START I (Strategic Arms Reduction Talks) treaty and to accede to the NPT. Some reports assert that Ukraine is seeking to gain operational control over the 176 strategic nuclear missiles on its territory, and that it could achieve this objective by mid- to late 1994.[16] Meanwhile, Ukraine's delay has led Russia and the United States to postpone implementation of the START treaties.

Of the former republics without nuclear weapons on their territories, the following have acceded to the NPT: Azerbaijan, Estonia, Latvia, Lithuania, and Uzbekistan. Of all the former Soviet republics, only Russia is a member of the Nuclear Suppliers Group.

Unsafeguarded nuclear facilities. Russia, as an NPT nuclear weapon state, is not required to keep its nuclear materials and facilities under safeguards. Facilities in other republics are subject to full-scope safeguards when the republics accede to the NPT and sign a safeguards agreement with the IAEA. Conventional wisdom has long maintained that facilities in the non-Russian republics do not pose an immediate indigenous proliferation threat because only Russia has operational sensitive facilities for the production of plutonium and highly enriched uranium. Other experts, however, warn that other facilities in the non-Russian republics present proliferation risks.[17] A fast breeder reactor in Kazakhstan, for example, is a potential source of plutonium, and nuclear materials on the Nuclear Suppliers Group trigger list are found at other facilities in non-Russian republics. Table 9.1 presents an overview of the nuclear assets of the former Soviet republics.

• India

India's initial pursuit of a nuclear explosive was driven by the nuclear capability of its northeastern neighbor, China. Current interest in stockpiling nuclear weapons, however, appears to be motivated by the nuclear ambitions of Pakistan, its western rival.

After its May 1974 peaceful nuclear explosion, India did not proceed to build a nuclear arsenal but appeared content to use the blast to boost its international prestige and to signal China of its new capability. As evidence mounted of Pakistan's quest for a nuclear bomb, however, various Indian leaders vowed to maintain nuclear superiority over Pakistan. Each report of an advance in Pakistani nuclear capabilities moved India a step closer to stockpiling nuclear weapons. By 1983, India was reportedly ready to resume nuclear testing as Pakistani advances continued.[18] In

Table 9.1 Nuclear Profiles of the Soviet Successor States

Country	Nuclear weapons	Nuclear power reactor	Nuclear research reactor	Nuclear weapons design	Uranium mining, milling	Uranium enrichment capability	Fuel fabrication facility	Plutonium production, handling	Heavy-water production	Other NSG-controlled material	Nuclear research center	Nuclear test site	Acceded to NPT	NSG member
Armenia		a							b		X			
Azerbaijan													X	
Belarus	X		X								X		c	
Estonia					X								X	
Georgia			d								X			
Kazakhstan	X	X	X		X		X	e		f	X	X		
Kyrgyzstan					X									
Latvia			X								X		X	
Lithuania		X											X	
Moldova														
Russia	X	X	X	X	X	X	X	X	X	X	X	X	X	X
Tadjikistan					X				X					
Turkmenistan														
Ukraine	X	X	X		X				X	g	X			
Uzbekistan			X		X	h					X		X	

Source: William C. Potter, *Nuclear Profiles of the Soviet Successor States* (Monterey, Calif.: Program for Nonproliferation Studies, Monterey Institute of International Studies, 1993).

a The two Armenian reactors were shut down in 1989 for safety reasons, but the Armenian government has announced its intent to restart them.

b Although one report of an Armenian heavy-water site has appeared in print, there has been no additional confirmation.

c The Belarusian Parliament approved accession to the NPT on February 4, 1993, but at the time of this writing had not deposited its instrument of accession.

d The IRT-M Tbilisi was shut down in 1990.

e A hot cell is reportedly located at the Semipalatinsk test site.

f The Ulbinsky Metallurgy Plant in Ust-Kamenogorsk produces beryllium and possibly zirconium.

g Zirconium, hafnium, and ion exchange resins are produced in Ukraine at the Pridneprovsky Chemical factory.

h A uranium enrichment facility, of at least an experimental nature, probably operated at Navoi in the 1970s and 1980s.

1985, India began to produce unsafeguarded plutonium in response to reports of further nuclear bomb–related testing in Pakistan.[19] In 1986, the two rivals announced within a day of each other their ability to enrich uranium to weapons grade. In that same year India is thought to have begun assembling and stockpiling nuclear weapons. Today the Indian nuclear arsenal is estimated at forty to sixty warheads.

Involvement in nuclear commerce. The Indian Atomic Energy Commission (IAEC) announced in February 1991 that India intended to become a low-cost alternative supplier of nuclear technologies to developing nations.[20] In subsequent months India offered to sell research reactors under IAEA safeguards to Algeria, Cuba, Egypt, Iran, and Syria,[21] and the chairman of the IAEC indicated that India was also willing to sell spent-fuel reprocessing plants.[22] India refuses to require full-scope safeguards, however, as a condition of export. It has withdrawn the offer of a research reactor for Iran under pressure from the U.S. government.

Attitude toward nonproliferation. India has declined Pakistan's suggestion that the two nations simultaneously sign the NPT, reasoning that such a move would not address the security threat it faces from China. (India may be willing to join the NPT as a nuclear weapon state, but the five traditional nuclear powers are unlikely to welcome such a proposal.[23]) India has also declined a U.S. proposal for a five-nation conference to create a nuclear weapon–free zone in South Asia. India and Pakistan have agreed, however, on one modest confidence-building measure: a pledge not to attack each other's nuclear facilities. The agreement was fully implemented in early 1992.

Unsafeguarded nuclear facilities. Some of India's nuclear facilities fall under IAEA safeguards, but the nation also maintains an unsafeguarded nuclear program, which includes the following facilities: the Madras I and II nuclear power plants, the Dhruva research reactor, and two plutonium reprocessing plants at Tarapur and at the Bhabha Atomic Research Center.[24]

• Iran

Iranian thinking on nuclear weapons is difficult to assess. In fall 1992, the U.S. Central Intelligence Agency concluded that Iran could develop nuclear weapons by the year 2000, but the intelligence community is said to be divided about Iranian intentions in the nuclear realm.[25] Rumors of Iranian interest in nuclear weapons surface regularly—the most spectacular alleging Iranian acquisition in early 1992 of two tactical nuclear warheads from the former Soviet republic of Kazakhstan—but concrete evidence of this interest is scarce.

The late Shah was said to have begun a nuclear weapons program, which was stopped, at least temporarily, after the 1979 Iranian revolution. Iran's defeat in its war with Iraq may have impelled Iran to resurrect the nuclear weapons program, despite its commitment under the NPT not to do so. How Iran would pursue a nuclear bomb, however, is unclear. The nation has few nuclear resources: a research reactor, two uncompleted and dormant power reactors at Bushehr, and a small calutron, which is not capable of enriching significant quantities of uranium. Although rumors persist of clandestine centrifuge enrichment plants under construction at Moallem Kalayah and at Karaj, no evidence of such facilities or of other infrastructure needed to produce a bomb has been found. Most observers believe that indigenous development of nuclear weapons would require more than a decade, and then only if a concerted effort were made.[26] A near-term Iranian nuclear bomb could be produced only with outside assistance.

Involvement in nuclear commerce. China agreed in 1990 to supply Iran with a research reactor and technical assistance at Isfahan. It has also transferred a small calutron to Iran, which in itself is not of immediate proliferation concern but could be reproduced in quantity to give Iran an enrichment capability. China built upon this relationship by clinching a deal to supply Iran with four reactors and a research center. Other nations have shown greater restraint with Iran. India was interested in selling a research reactor to Iran, but bowed to U.S. pressure and canceled the deal. Pakistan is rumored to be assisting an Iranian bomb program, but U.S. officials confirm that Pakistan recently refused an Iranian request to purchase key weapons components. Of perhaps greater concern are reports of Iranian procurement fronts attempting to purchase dual-use or sensitive nuclear technologies from German firms. This is the approach Iraq used in its bid for nuclear weapons.[27]

Attitude toward nonproliferation. Iran is a party to the NPT, but statements from the Iranian leadership cast doubt on the nation's commitment to nonproliferation. In October 1988, Rafsanjani, then speaker of the Iranian parliament, declared that Iran should seek an atomic military capability, and as recently as October 1991 an Iranian vice-president asserted that Muslim nations should work to develop a nuclear bomb as long as Israel has one.[28] On the other hand, IAEA officials, including Director General Hans Blix, found no cause for concern in the Iranian program following a February 1992 visit to Iran. The visit, however, was not regarded as an inspection.

Unsafeguarded nuclear facilities. All known nuclear facilities requiring safeguards under the NPT are currently safeguarded.

• *Iraq*

The secret Iraqi nuclear program illustrates the need for a strong nonproliferation regime. The nation had developed a vast hidden nuclear infrastructure dedicated to the development of a nuclear bomb, including facilities for various kinds of uranium enrichment. Most disturbing, it was able to do so while maintaining the appearance of a faithful NPT party.

The Iraqi quest for a nuclear bomb goes back to the 1970s when Iraq imported the Osiraq reactor from France. Ostensibly a research reactor, Osiraq was relatively large (40 MW), raising suspicions that it would be used for plutonium production. In 1981, Iraq was preparing to submit the nearly finished reactor to IAEA inspections, as required by the NPT, when it was bombed by the Israeli air force. Israel apparently had little faith that IAEA safeguards would deter development of an Iraqi nuclear weapon.

Destruction of the reactor did not end Iraq's pursuit of a nuclear weapons capability. In the mid- to late 1980s Baghdad began an aggressive and often secret campaign to acquire the technology needed to support a nuclear weapons program. It is estimated to have dedicated 10,000 scientists and technicians and $10 billion to the effort.[29] By the time of the Gulf War, Iraq was thought to be within two to three years of a nuclear weapons capability.

Involvement in nuclear commerce. Iraq's strategy for acquiring sensitive nuclear technologies was to purchase components and subunits of these technologies rather than entire facilities. In this way, Iraq could more plausibly claim that a given item was destined for an innocuous civilian project. In the 1980s, Iraq sought materials and equipment for its centrifuge and calutron enrichment programs, as well as for warhead development. Centrifuge equipment was purchased from U.S., German, and Swiss firms, among others. Calutron equipment has been more difficult to trace, but some appears to have been supplied unknowingly by Austria. Firms and individuals from Switzerland, Japan, Chile, and Germany appear to have been involved in exports instrumental in the weapons configuration aspect of the Iraqi program.[30]

Attitude toward nonproliferation. The Iraqi underground nuclear program violated Iraq's NPT-mandated pledge not to seek nuclear weapons, as well as its safeguards obligations under the treaty. Throughout the course of the UN Special Commission inspections of Iraq, the Baghdad government was frequently uncooperative and less than frank in its revelation of Iraqi capabilities. Its final report on the Iraqi nuclear program is believed to be incomplete. Iraqi obstinance continued into 1993 when Iraq refused to allow UN inspectors into certain facilities.

Unsafeguarded nuclear facilities. Much of Iraq's nuclear infrastructure was destroyed during the Gulf War or as part of the inspections of the UN Special Commission. Iraq is not known to have additional unsafeguarded nuclear facilities, but the government's history of underreporting its capabilities casts doubt on this conclusion.

• Israel

Israel was the first state to adopt a long-term policy of refusing to acknowledge its possession of a nuclear weapons stockpile. Today, more than two decades after Israel gained a nuclear weapons capability, it still avoids publicly recognizing this military milestone.

Israel's nuclear weapons program dates back to 1956 when France secretly agreed to sell Israel a research reactor and spent-fuel reprocessing plant. (These facilities, located at Dimona, are still at the heart of Israel's nuclear warhead production program.) Thirty years of speculation about Israel's nuclear plans gave way in 1986 to hard evidence of nuclear weapons development when a former technician at the Dimona plant revealed the existence of plutonium extraction and weapons fabrication capabilities underground at the Dimona site. The technician's information provided strong evidence that the Israeli nuclear stockpile was both larger and more powerful than observers had guessed. Total warheads were estimated at between one and two hundred, rather than the twenty to twenty-five previously believed to constitute Israel's inventory, and Israel's use of tritium allowed it to boost the yield of some of its warheads to forty to fifty kilotons each. Some estimate today's Israeli nuclear stockpile at several hundred warheads.

Involvement in nuclear commerce. Israel is not a significant nuclear exporter. Its checkered history as an importer has included smuggling activity (nuclear triggers) as well as incomplete accounting of the use of imported materials (heavy water from Norway). Other nuclear technologies have been imported secretly, such as the Dimona reactor and reprocessing technology purchased from France.

Attitude toward nonproliferation. Israel has long maintained that it will not be the first to introduce nuclear weapons into the Middle East, an ambiguous statement designed to preserve Israeli nuclear options. In 1981, Prime Minister Menachem Begin added another maxim to Israeli nonproliferation policy when he declared that Israel would not allow any hostile state to develop nuclear weapons.[31] The declaration followed the Israeli bombing of the Osiraq reactor in Iraq, which was suspected of supporting an Iraqi nuclear weapons program. Further revision of the Israeli stance, and evidence of a greater willingness to use nuclear weapons, was apparent by the late 1980s when Israel hinted on several occasions that its response to a chemical weapons attack would be "one hundred times stronger."[32]

Israel has responded to a May 1991 U.S. proposal for an end to fissile material production throughout the Middle East by saying that it is willing to discuss nuclear weapons in conjunction with chemical and conventional weapons, but will not discuss nuclear weapons alone.[33] Under the plan Israel would open its Dimona facilities to international inspection as the first step toward a nuclear weapon–free zone in the Middle East.

Unsafeguarded nuclear facilities. Nearly all of Israel's nuclear facilities are unsafeguarded. The Dimona complex, which includes a research reactor as well as plants for uranium conversion, uranium purification, fuel fabrication, spent-fuel reprocessing, and tritium production, is not subject to safeguards of any kind. Only the U.S.-supplied research reactor at Nahal Soreq was sold under safeguards.

• North Korea

North Korea's March 1993 announcement that it intended to withdraw from the NPT represents a significant setback for the nonproliferation regime. North Korea reacted in the face of an impending IAEA special inspection of two facilities near the Yongbyon nuclear research center suspected of supporting a North Korean nuclear weapons program. Its move was also meant as a protest of joint U.S.–South Korean military exercises under way at the time. Although North Korea left the door open to a reversal of its action "when the U.S. nuclear threats and the unjust conduct of the IAEA against the DPRK"[34] are removed, the North showed no sign of budging in subsequent negotiations with the United States over the issue.

The North's nuclear program dates as far back as possibly 1972.[35] That year, after three decades of bitter relations with South Korea, Pyongyang began construction of a 30-MW research reactor at Yongbyon. The plant's relatively large size (most research reactors are less than 5 MW[36]) would enable it to yield enough plutonium annually for one atomic bomb. Without a reprocessing facility to extract plutonium from the reactor's spent fuel, however, the plant was not an immediate proliferation threat. Moreover, North Korea's accession to the NPT in 1985 meant that the facility would be subject to inspections as soon as the treaty-mandated IAEA safeguards agreement was signed. In sum, North Korea did not appear to pose a significant proliferation risk in 1985.

Two subsequent North Korean actions, however, raised suspicions regarding the direction of its nuclear policy. Between 1985 and 1992 Pyongyang found a variety of pretexts for refusing to sign the NPT-mandated safeguards agreement with the IAEA. These excuses ranged from technical errors in the original IAEA-supplied document to the continued presence of U.S. nuclear weapons in South Korea. No sooner was one North Korean concern resolved than another was presented, giving the impression that Pyongyang was stalling for time to advance its nuclear capability before submitting to inspections.

The objective of these delaying tactics was clarified in 1989 when U.S. satellites photographed construction of a reprocessing plant next to the Yongbyon reactor. A reprocessing plant, combined with the recently completed oversized research reactor and North Korea's repeated delays in signing a safeguards agreement, seemed to indicate the nation's intention to produce weapons-grade nuclear material, presumably for a bomb program. Intense diplomatic pressure from the United States, the Soviet Union, Japan, and the IAEA in the next two years led Pyongyang to end its policy of procrastination. In April 1992, after the United States and South Korea assured North Korea that it faced no nuclear weapons in the South, and after the two Koreas signed a joint declaration proscribing nuclear weapons development and the construction of reprocessing and enrichment plants, North Korea finalized its commitment to inspections.[37] The first of these took place in May 1992. When the IAEA insisted in March 1993 on inspecting the suspected nuclear facilities near Yongbyon, however, the North gave notice of its intent to leave the NPT. It "suspended" its withdrawal in June 1993, but continued to refuse the IAEA access to the suspected facilities.

Involvement in nuclear commerce. North Korea has not been a significant exporter of nuclear material, although its uranium reportedly has been exported to the People's Republic of China and the former Soviet Union.

Attitude toward nonproliferation. As noted above, North Korea's commitment to nonproliferation has been less than complete. Its withdrawal from the NPT and its refusal to allow further inspections raise serious doubts about the peaceful nature of its nuclear program.

Unsafeguarded nuclear facilities. The IAEA maintained in March 1993 that the safeguards agreement with North Korea remained in force. North Korea, however, has not allowed further inspections of its facilities, which can no longer be considered to be safeguarded.

• Pakistan

Pakistan's defeat in the 1971 Indo-Pakistani war apparently convinced Islamabad of the need for a nuclear weapons capability. To this end, Pakistan attempted throughout the 1970s to acquire a plutonium reprocessing plant from France and components for a uranium enrichment facility from a variety of sources. The former effort was squelched when the U.S. government persuaded France of the proliferation concerns surrounding export of the plant. The uranium enrichment plant, however, was constructed at Kahuta following a persistent smuggling campaign, which yielded plant designs and components from Western firms.

Throughout the 1980s, the case of Pakistan forced the United States to choose between incompatible foreign policy goals: on the one hand, the United States sought to retain Pakistan as a strategic ally, particularly to counter Soviet expansionism in Afghanistan; on the other, it wanted to curb the increasingly clear Pakistani appetite for a nuclear weapons capability. Time and again in the 1980s the United States ruled in favor of the effort to contain the Soviet Union, and turned a blind eye to Pakistani nuclear activities. These activities included the 1984 attempt to smuggle nuclear weapons triggers out of the United States, the 1985 decision to enrich uranium to a level higher than 5 percent in contravention of agreements with the United States, and the 1987 declaration by a high Pakistani nuclear official that Pakistan had produced weapons-grade uranium. The U.S. policy removed some of the disincentives for development of Pakistan's nuclear arsenal, estimated at ten to fifteen devices.[38]

Involvement in nuclear commerce. Pakistan has been an active nuclear importer and has been willing to use secret or illegal means to gain access to the materials and technologies it desires. In addition to the smuggling of nuclear triggers mentioned above, Pakistan attempted in 1987 to smuggle enrichment and tritium production technology from West Germany and maraging steel from the United States. Islamabad reportedly received nuclear weapons design assistance from China in the 1980s. Pakistan has also been mentioned as a nuclear supplier in recent years, specifically with regard to the retransfer to Iran, Iraq, and North Korea of uranium enrichment equipment received from West Germany.

Attitude toward nonproliferation. Pakistan announced in February 1992 that it possessed the wherewithal to build a nuclear bomb, but said it would not do so, and claimed to have frozen its nuclear program.[39] Pakistan has proposed a number of arms control measures to reduce tensions with India, including simultaneous accession to the NPT by both nations, establishment of a nuclear weapon–free zone in the region, mutual agreement not to manufacture nuclear arms, and mutual acceptance of IAEA safeguards on all nuclear facilities.[40] India has rejected these proposals.

Unsafeguarded nuclear facilities. Many of Pakistan's nuclear installations, including several sensitive facilities, are not safeguarded.

Among these facilities are the uranium conversion plant at Dera Ghazi Khan; the heavy-water production plant at Multan; the uranium enrichment plants at Kahuta, Sihala, and Golra; the fuel fabrication plant at Chashma; and the tritium purification plant south of Rawalpindi.[41] The reprocessing plant at Chashma is expected to be subject to safeguards.

• South Africa

South Africa, like Brazil and Argentina, represents one of several nonproliferation regime "success stories" of the early 1990s. South Africa reversed direction in its nuclear program when it signed the NPT and submitted its nuclear facilities to IAEA inspections in 1991. In fact, President F. W. de Klerk revealed in March 1993 that South Africa had pursued development of a nuclear arsenal until 1990, and had actually produced six nuclear weapons. The weapons were meant to serve as a deterrent and to "persuade nuclear weapon states, especially the United States, to intervene on its behalf" in case of a crisis in Southern Africa.[42] In 1990, he said, the program was terminated and the weapons destroyed. South Africa thus became the first nation ever to abolish its entire nuclear arsenal.

The South African program dates back to the mid-1960s, when government officials spoke of the need to preserve South Africa's nuclear option and refused to sign the NPT. Pretoria then began construction in the early 1970s of a small enrichment plant at Valindaba, which is said to have produced the highly enriched uranium used in South Africa's nuclear program.

Evidence of South Africa's interest in nuclear weapons was uncovered in 1977 when satellites spotted a nuclear weapons test site under construction in South Africa's Kalahari Desert. Pretoria was persuaded to dismantle the site, but not necessarily to abandon pursuit of testing: just two years later satellites detected a flash of light over the South Atlantic in the distinctive pattern of a nuclear test. Many experts believe the flash resulted from a joint South African–Israeli nuclear test, although South Africa has denied this and asserts that its nuclear weapons program was developed without outside help.

By 1981 South Africa was capable of enriching uranium to 45 percent, a level from which little additional work is needed to raise the uranium to weapons-grade. By 1988 South African officials were claiming that the nation was capable of manufacturing nuclear weapons.

In 1989 changes in South Africa's security, political, and diplomatic environments made possible a shift in its nuclear policy. Cuba had agreed to pull its troops from Angola, the Soviet presence in the region was diminishing, a change in leadership brought new thinking to Pretoria, and IAEA member states continued to threaten South Africa's expulsion from the IAEA. These incentives led South Africa in January 1990 to close the enrichment plant that had produced the highly enriched uranium for its weapons program, and to announce in September that it would sign the NPT if other Southern African nations did so as well.

Involvement in nuclear commerce. South Africa has long been a supplier of natural and processed uranium, but is not known to have exported much nuclear technology. It is said to have supplied weapons-grade uranium to Israel in return for missile technology, and the two nations may have worked together on nuclear weapons development.

Attitude toward nonproliferation. South Africa acceded to the NPT in July 1991 and signed a safeguards agreement with the IAEA shortly thereafter. Some nations fear that, despite its March 1993 nuclear confession, South Africa may not have revealed to the IAEA the full extent of its nuclear assets, in order to preserve a cache of nuclear weapons or nuclear weapons materials. There is little evidence, however, to substantiate these fears.

Unsafeguarded nuclear facilities. South Africa apparently is fulfilling its commitment to place all peaceful nuclear activities under safeguards. As the first nation to divest itself entirely of nuclear weapons, however, the South African case raises interesting questions of accountability: how can the IAEA be sure that it knows about and is safeguarding *all* South African fissile material? The agency is meeting this challenge in part by using historical production information to develop estimates of fissile material production in South Africa over the past decade. These estimates are then compared with the inventory of fissile material declared to the IAEA by South Africa in October 1991. As of summer 1993, small discrepancies between the IAEA's estimate and South Africa's declared inventory were being investigated. The discrepancies, however, may be attributed to inaccurate or nonexistent records of waste assays from the production process.[43] Most observers appear not to be concerned that South Africa is hiding significant quantities of nuclear material.

NOTES

1. George Church, "Who Else Will Have the Bomb," *Time* (December 16, 1991), p. 48.

2. "Algeria Agrees to Safeguard Suspect Reactor," *Arms Control Today* (May 1992), p. 25.

3. Ibid.

4. Leonard Spector with Jacqueline Smith, *Nuclear Ambitions: The Spread of Nuclear Weapons 1989–1990* (Boulder, Colo.: Westview Press, 1990), p. 224.

5. Leonard S. Spector, *A Historical and Technical Introduction to the Proliferation of Nuclear Weapons* (Washington, D.C.: Carnegie Endowment for International Peace, 1992), p. 22

6. Jon B. Wolfsthal, "Argentina Ships Condor Missiles for Destruction, Joins MTCR," *Arms Control Today* (April 1993), p. 24.

7. *Eye on Supply* (Winter 1993), p. 50.

8. *Eye on Supply* (Winter 1993), pp. 47–48.

9. William C. Potter, "Nuclear Exports from the Former Soviet Union: What's New, What's True," *Arms Control Today* (January/February 1993), p. 3.

10. Roger Fallgot and Ian Mather, "Iran Has the N-Bomb," *The European* (April 30–May 3, 1992), p. 1.

11. "Soviet Nuclear Warheads to Iran?" *Trust and Verify* (April 1992), p. 1.

12. See Matthew Campbell, "Russians Storm Jet to Stop Korean Bomb," *Sunday Times* (London), December 20, 1992, for an account of alleged attempts by nuclear and rocket scientists to emigrate to North Korea.

13. Potter, pp. 3–4.

14. Ibid.

15. *Arms Control Reporter*, p. 602.B.239, April 1993.

16. Michael R. Gordon, "With Aid, U.S. Seeks to Sway Ukraine on A-Arms," *New York Times*, June 4, 1993, p. A7.

17. See William C. Potter, *Nuclear Profiles of the Soviet Successor States* (Monterey, Calif.: Program for Nonproliferation Studies, Monterey Institute of International Studies, 1993).

18. Spector and Smith, p. 65.

19. Ibid., p. 66.

20. "India Will Actively Seek to Export Nuclear Technology," *Nuclear News* (March 1991), p. 56.

21. *Eye on Supply*, (6: Spring 1992), pp. 9–10.

22. "Joint U.S. Nonproliferation Talks Needed," *Proliferation Issues* (August 21, 1991), p. 11. Original source: C. Raja Mohan, "Nonproliferation: New Perceptions," *The Hindu* (Madras), July 18, 1991, p. 8.

23. "PRC Decision on Nonproliferation Pact Welcomed," *Proliferation Issues* (September 27, 1991), p. 14. Original source: *Patriot* (New Delhi), August 12, 1991, p. 5.

24. Spector and Smith, p. 65.

25. *New York Times*, November 30, 1993, p. A1.

26. David Albright and Mark Hibbs, "Spotlight Shifts to Iran," *Bulletin of the Atomic Scientists* (March 1992), p. 11.

27. *Eye on Supply* (Winter 1993), p. 10.

28. Elaine Sciolino, "Intelligence Report Indicates Iran Has Been Seeking Nuclear Arms," *New York Times*, October 31, 1991, p. A9.

29. Joseph Nye, "New Approaches to Nuclear Nonproliferation Policy," *Science* (May 29, 1992), p. 1294.

30. David Albright and Mark Hibbs, "Iraq's Shop-Till-You-Drop Nuclear Program," *Bulletin of the Atomic Scientists* (April 1992), p. 37.

31. Glenn Frankel, "Iraq Said Developing A-Weapons," *Washington Post*, March 31, 1989, p. A32.

32. See Leonard S. Spector, "Nonproliferation—After the Bomb Has Spread," *Arms Control Today* (December 1988), p. 10.

33. "Dimona et al." *Economist* (March 14, 1992), p. 46.

34. "North Korea's Diplomatic Bombshell," *Arms Control Today* (April 1993), p. 22.

35. Daniel K. Shultz and Betsy C. Perabo, "North Korean Nuclear Developments: An Updated Chronology," Emerging Nuclear Suppliers Project, Monterey Institute of International Studies, June 1, 1993, p. 2.

36. C. Walters, personal correspondence, July 15, 1992.

37. Leonard S. Spector, *A Historical and Technical Introduction to the Proliferation of Nuclear Weapons* (Washington, D.C.: Carnegie Endowment for International Peace, 1992), p. 36.

38. Spector, p. 31.

39. Paul Lewis, "Pakistan Tells of Its A-Bomb Capacity," *New York Times*, February 8, 1992, p. A5.

40. Spector and Smith, p. 98.

41. Ibid., pp. 114–115.

42. Jon B. Wolfsthal, "South Africa Reveals It Had Six Nuclear Weapons Until 1990," *Arms Control Today* (April 1993), p. 23.

43. David Albright, "A Proliferation Primer," *Bulletin of the Atomic Scientists,* June 1993, p. 20.

10

Current Challenges to the Nonproliferation Regime

The nuclear nonproliferation regime is stronger than ever, but it continues to face a series of challenges. This chapter provides a survey of outstanding issues facing the regime, as well as proposed solutions for dealing with them.

THE GLUT OF FISSILE MATERIALS

Global stocks of plutonium and highly enriched uranium are at an all-time high and continue to increase. A total of 100 tons of separated plutonium is expected to accumulate in Japan, Germany, Belgium, and Switzerland by the end of the twentieth century.[1] Because less than 10 kg of plutonium is needed to build a nuclear explosive, the proliferation risks associated with such large quantities of bomb material cannot be overstated.

Excess civilian stocks of plutonium are a legacy of policies set decades ago, when breeder reactors were expected eventually to dominate the nuclear reactor world because of their potential to produce virtually inexhaustible supplies of nuclear fuel. Although breeders are nearly self-sufficient in producing fresh plutonium fuel, they require large initial stocks of plutonium for start-up. To this end, nations intent on following a breeder reactor strategy began to stockpile plutonium extracted from spent fuel, rather than discard spent fuel as reactor waste.

The breeder reactor, however, has turned out to be an uneconomical technology, and it is not expected to reach full development until the next century, if ever. As a consequence, large plutonium stocks in some nations have no apparent short-term purpose. The problem is especially acute in Japan, which in 1993 began receiving plutonium extracted in France and the United Kingdom from Japanese spent-fuel rods. This stockpile, combined with the plutonium from Japan's own reprocessing plants, by the 2020s will total more than all the plutonium used by the superpowers in their tens of thousands of nuclear warheads.[2] Stocks of this magnitude

would make disposal of excess stocks by the superpowers politically difficult, and could lead other nations to seek fissile material stockpiles.

The problem of surplus fissile material also has military roots. The
vast reductions in warheads called for under U.S.-Russian arms agreements are beginning to produce large stockpiles of plutonium and enriched
uranium. This stockpile is expected to increase substantially throughout
the 1990s, as the number of warheads is slashed by more than half from
their 1990 levels.

The safe storage of this growing volume of fissile material poses a
tremendous challenge for the regime. Several proposals for the disposal of
surplus fissile material are under consideration. One calls for storage of
the materials under international auspices, an idea first proposed in the
Baruch Plan of 1946. Although the plan was never adopted, the IAEA was
given authority in its 1957 statutes to serve as an international repository
of fissile material. This authority has never been invoked, but could be a
suitable solution to the problem of surplus fissile materials disposal.

Another possible solution to the fissile materials glut is to burn the material in existing reactors. Fuel made of a mixture of plutonium and uranium,
known as mixed-oxide (MOX) fuel, can be used to run many reactors. Alternatively, plutonium could be burned in fast breeder reactors modified to
become fast burners. The Japanese government, which has said it does not
want to accumulate plutonium, is considering both of these alternatives.[3]

ADEQUACY OF SAFEGUARDS

IAEA safeguards came under attack following the 1991 revelations of a
massive nuclear program in Iraq, an NPT signatory whose peaceful nuclear program is subject to full-scope safeguards. That nation's multibil-
lion dollar nuclear effort was carried out even as IAEA inspectors found
no evidence of illegal activity at declared Iraqi facilities. The Iraqi case
raised serious concerns about the efficacy of IAEA inspections.

The truth is that IAEA safeguards are as effective as member-states
allow them to be. The agency was not negligent in its handling of the Iraqi
inspections, but was kept on a short safeguarding leash by IAEA member-
states. The Iraqi revelations, however, generated interest in increasing the
safeguarding authority of the agency.

Several proposals for strengthening the IAEA's safeguarding authority were advanced in 1991–1992. One was to adopt random, rather than
scheduled, inspections. Under this plan, the agency would devise a system
whereby inspection visits would be carried out irregularly, rather than at
set intervals as current safeguards agreements dictate. However, the random inspections would be announced in advance, eliminating the element
of surprise and reducing the inspections' effectiveness.

Another reform involves more frequent use of special inspections by the IAEA. Special inspections are inspections that are neither regularly scheduled nor limited to facilities listed in the agency's safeguards agreement with the state. In 1992, the board of governors reaffirmed the right of the agency's director general to initiate special inspections without obtaining the permission of the board of governors. However, the IAEA is not likely to aggressively employ its special inspections authority. The issue remains politically sensitive, and only judicious use of the special inspections power is likely to be tolerated by agency member-states. Moreover, some elements in the U.S. government are reported to favor the transfer of inspection authority from the IAEA to the UN Security Council, where the United States has greater influence.[4]

One relatively modest reform that appears to be gaining widespread acceptance is the early reporting to the IAEA of design information on nuclear facilities planned or under construction. Currently, facility design specifications are delivered to the agency just prior to the introduction of fissile material. Such late notification prevents the agency from influencing facility design in such a way as to make the facility "safeguards friendly." As noted in Chapter 6, the IAEA's board of governors voted in February 1992 to urge early reporting of construction information. The reform is backed by several European Community nations as well as Japan and Canada.

NUCLEAR TESTING AND NUCLEAR DISARMAMENT

Non–nuclear weapon states have long regarded nuclear testing as the touchstone of nuclear weapon states' commitment to nonproliferation. The end of the Cold War has reinforced this sentiment, and pressure on NWS to end testing is evident. Russia announced in October 1991 a one-year moratorium on testing, and France followed suit in summer 1992. The United States and the United Kingdom have long claimed that continued testing is necessary to ensure the safety of nuclear explosives, but the U.S. Congress appears increasingly firm about pursuing a comprehensive test ban. It legislated a nine-month test ban in September 1992 (effectively halting UK tests as well, which are carried out at the U.S. testing site in Nevada). The moratorium was extended into 1994 by President Clinton, on the condition that no other nations renew testing. China, however, has not committed itself to any moratorium. Renewed testing by China could halt the momentum for a CTB that has developed since the end of the Cold War.[5]

Some observers fear that the regime could unravel if NWS do not commit themselves to end nuclear testing. Such a commitment was demanded by a group of NNWS at the 1990 NPT review conference, and the issue will likely resurface at the 1995 NPT extension conference. While treaty extension is probably not threatened by the test ban issue, the terms of extension could be affected by it, as could the worldwide commitment to the norms of the nonproliferation regime.

PROLIFERATION POTENTIAL OF THE FORMER SOVIET UNION

The dissolution of the Soviet Union is a major potential proliferation problem. Russia appears to be continuing the prudent nonproliferation policies of the USSR, but faces serious challenges in accounting for and disposing of the large quantities of plutonium and highly enriched uranium from warheads to be dismantled in this decade. In addition, the nonproliferation positions of the other republics remain untested and, in some cases, undeveloped, although the key states of Belarus, Kazakhstan, and Ukraine declared in 1992 their intention to sign the NPT as non–nuclear weapon states "at an early date."

Of greater concern than their attitude toward nonproliferation is the export position of the non-Russian republics. These states have little experience in export control administration, and may not have the mechanisms needed to seal their borders from nuclear technology leakage. Even prior to the official breakup of the former Soviet Union, in the fall of 1991, Soviet plutonium and enriched uranium were being smuggled through Europe, and unconfirmed reports since then allege that two nuclear weapons were transferred from Kazakhstan to Iran.

The long-feared emigration of nuclear scientists from the former Soviet Union to nations of proliferation concern is another area requiring attention. In spring 1992, the United States, Germany, the European Community, and other governments agreed to establish scientific centers in the former Soviet republics to offer meaningful employment to scientists there, but the centers had not gained approval from the Russian or Ukraine parliaments as of mid-1993, and have not begun operation. Underused scientific talent may also be absorbed by Western firms for research work, either in the West, or more frequently, in the former Soviet republics. Although little evidence exists of significant emigration from the former Soviet Union, it is unclear whether these measures will be sufficient to ensure that nuclear know-how in the former Soviet republics is not transferred abroad.

INEFFECTIVE IMPLEMENTATION OF EXPORT CONTROLS

Many nations have accepted the need for greater control over nuclear exports, but their capacity to enforce export control laws often remains in doubt. Effective enforcement requires adequate staffing and funding, both of which may be in short supply in emerging nuclear supplier nations. Also in short supply may be the political will to follow through on new export control commitments. In some nations the political leadership may face bureaucratic resistance to tighter controls, and with little perceived political benefit from insisting on greater enforcement, newly enacted export control legislation may be allowed to lie dormant. Technical assistance from traditional supplier nations may be necessary to help export control agencies in new supplier nations track and regulate a longer list of controlled items.

The problem is not limited to nations new to the nuclear export field, however. Much of the gas centrifuge enrichment technology imported by Iraq was on trigger lists but slipped through the export control mechanisms of the most experienced nuclear exporters, including France, Germany, the United Kingdom, and the United States. Greater attention to enforcement of export control laws is necessary in many nations.

DRAWING NEW PARTICIPANTS INTO THE REGIME

Perhaps the most difficult problem facing the nonproliferation regime is persuading nations outside or partly outside the formal regime structures to embrace regime norms. Aside from signing the NPT, the following steps could help bring nonparticipant nations into the nonproliferation fold.

1. Creation of nuclear weapon–free zones. The establishment of nuclear weapon–free zones in the Middle East and South Asia would draw key states into the regime and help defuse tensions in critical regions. As a tentative step toward a NWFZ in the Middle East, the 1991 IAEA General Conference voted to draft a model full-scope safeguards agreement for use in the Middle East. Israel, however, is expected to resist such a move. A U.S.-proposed five-nation conference on an NWFZ in South Asia has sparked some interest in that region, although India has serious reservations about the proposal.

2. Adoption of full-scope safeguards export policy. Emerging nuclear supplier nations should be urged to join the Nuclear Suppliers Group or, at a minimum, to adopt the new NSG policy requiring full-scope safeguards as a condition of export. Non-NSG nations capable of exporting nuclear technology include Argentina, Brazil, China, India, Israel, Pakistan, South Africa, South Korea, and Taiwan. Bringing all nuclear suppliers in line on full-scope safeguards would severely curtail opportunities for diversion of imported nuclear materials and technology to military purposes.

3. Elimination of sensitive nuclear exports. Another NSG policy worthy of emulation is the embargo on the export of sensitive nuclear technology such as enrichment or reprocessing plants. Denial of such technology would eliminate the most direct options for production of weapons-grade fissile material.

PROLIFERATION OF OLD TECHNOLOGIES

In the face of increasingly strict controls on nuclear exports, nations interested in developing nuclear weapons may turn to uncontrolled, antiquated technology to obtain the facilities they lack. This problem came to light when it was revealed that Iraq had used an outdated technology called a calutron to enrich uranium. The calutron was developed by the United States during World War II and has long been overlooked as a proliferation threat. Until Iraq's use of this technology was revealed, in fact, the calutron was not subject to export controls.[6]

NOTES

1. Lawrence Scheinman and David Fischer, "Managing the Glut of Nuclear Weapon Materials," *Arms Control Today* (March 1992), p. 8.

2. Michael Cross, "Japan's Plutonium Stockpile," *New Scientist* (February 1, 1992), p. 10.

3. Naoaki Usui and Ann Maclachlan, "Turn Breeders to Burners? Idea Catching On in Japan, Europe," *Nucleonics Week* (April 30, 1992), pp. 5–6.

4. The Pentagon, the CIA, and parts of the State Department are said to favor a Security Council inspectorate, whereas the Department of Energy, parts of the State Department, and much of the Congress favor maintaining inspections authority in the IAEA. L. Scheinman, personal correspondence, July 16, 1992. See also Mark Hibbs, "Special Inspections: A Transatlantic Turf War for Post-Iraq Powers," *Nucleonics Week* (January 30, 1992), pp. 14–15.

5. Douglas Jehl, "Clinton Expected to Order Renewal of Nuclear Tests," *New York Times,* May 15, 1993, p. A1.

6. Sean Tyson, "Uranium Enrichment Technologies: Proliferation Implications," *Eye on Supply* (Fall 1991), p. 79.

11

Summary

The nuclear nonproliferation regime encompasses a series of complex issues. The most important of these are summarized below.

ON NUCLEAR FISSION

- Atomic energy, whether in a nuclear reactor or in a nuclear bomb, is produced when atoms are split apart (fission) or fused together (fusion).
- Fissile material is needed to produce a nuclear bomb. One natural isotope, U-235, and two manufactured ones, Pu-239 and U-233, are fissile.
- These fissile materials, highly enriched uranium and plutonium, are highly sensitive.

ON THE NUCLEAR FUEL CYCLE

- The most sensitive nuclear facilities are uranium enrichment and plutonium reprocessing plants.
- *In isolation*, other nuclear facilities do not pose a great proliferation threat.
- Nuclear power plants are a proliferation concern if (1) they use plutonium or highly enriched uranium or (2) if they are used in conjunction with a plutonium reprocessing facility.
- A plutonium fuel cycle, in which nuclear fuel is reprocessed and recycled, presents greater proliferation dangers than a "once-through" fuel cycle. This is because weapons-usable plutonium is present at various points in the plutonium fuel cycle.

ON THE HISTORY OF THE NONPROLIFERATION REGIME

- Although great restrictions were envisioned in the regime's earliest days, these gave way to a looser arrangement under which access to nuclear materials and technology was granted in exchange for safeguards on nuclear facilities or materials.
- Nonproliferation treaties, especially the Non-Proliferation Treaty of 1970, have played a pivotal role in stemming the spread of nuclear weapons.
- Restrictions on nuclear exports have grown tighter over time. Whereas a nuclear aspirant in the 1950s and 1960s could import entire sensitive facilities, today's aspirant must rely on the smuggling or importing of facility components or dual-use items to build a clandestine nuclear capability.
- The nuclear nonproliferation regime is more influential today than ever before.

ON SAFEGUARDS

- None of the many types of international nuclear safeguards directly prevents the diversion of fissile material to illicit uses. Instead, they alert the global community about a diversion.
- Full-scope safeguards cover all fissile material in a nation, no matter what its source. Item-only safeguards are applied only to a particular item.

ON THE POLITICS OF NONPROLIFERATION

- The historical record indicates that the spread of nuclear weapons is not inevitable.
- Nations seeking a nuclear weapons capability are typically motivated by a perceived need for greater security, although prestige, domestic pressures, and other factors may also play a role.
- Factors dissuading a nation from pursuing a nuclear weapons capability include the insecurity resulting from possession of a vulnerable nuclear arsenal, the growing international disapproval of the acquisition of nuclear arms, domestic and bureaucratic pressures, or the fear of economic or military sanctions.

ON THE NPT REVIEW CONFERENCE

- Delegates to the NPT Extension Conference will decide on the length of NPT extension. The NPT does not offer delegates the option to vote directly to terminate the treaty.

- However, if delegates vote to extend the NPT for a single fixed period (of whatever length), the treaty would terminate at the end of that period.

ON NATIONS OF PROLIFERATION CONCERN

- Aside from the five NPT-recognized nuclear weapon states (the United States, Russia, the United Kingdom, France, and China), the following nations are known or believed to have a nuclear explosive capability: India (detonated a "peaceful nuclear explosive" in 1974), Israel (believed to have manufactured and stockpiled several hundred nuclear weapons), South Africa (possibly conducted a joint nuclear explosive test with Israel in 1979), and Pakistan (announced in 1992 its ability to manufacture a nuclear explosive).
- Iraq actively pursued a nuclear weapons capability before the 1991 Gulf War. It is believed to continue to harbor nuclear ambitions.
- Iran and Algeria are suspected of having covert nuclear weapons programs, but the evidence of this, especially in the case of Algeria, is scant.
- Argentina, Brazil, and North Korea have all forsworn nuclear weapons ambitions. All were suspected of coveting nuclear weapons in the 1980s, and Brazil admitted to having pursued a secret nuclear weapons program.
- China's record of nuclear exports is blemished. Pressure on state ministries to earn hard currency has led to imprudent nuclear sales even as official Chinese rhetoric on nonproliferation has grown stronger.
- The republics of the former Soviet Union could become sources of nuclear materials, technology, know-how, and possibly weapons for overseas customers. Export control mechanisms are not well developed, and the nonproliferation commitment of many of the republics is unknown or untested.

ON CURRENT ISSUES IN THE NONPROLIFERATION REGIME

- A glut of plutonium and enriched uranium is expected globally by the end of the century. No plan for the use or disposal of this material has been agreed upon.
- International safeguards need to be strengthened.
- Continued nuclear weapons testing by nuclear weapon states could be a source of contention in the 1990s, particularly with the end of the Cold War. The issue could affect the terms on which the NPT is extended in 1995.

- Tighter interstate borders and strong nonproliferation commitments are needed in the republics of the former Soviet Union.
- The nuclear nonproliferation regime must be made as universal as possible. Efforts must be made to include those nations that are currently of greatest proliferation concern.
- A review of the export control status of antiquated nuclear technologies is needed to help prevent their clandestine acquisition.

Appendix:
Treaty on the
Non-Proliferation of
Nuclear Weapons

Signed at London, Moscow, and Washington, July 1, 1968
Entered into Force, March 5, 1970

The States concluding this Treaty, hereinafter referred to as the "Parties to the Treaty,"

Considering the devastation that would be visited upon all mankind by a nuclear war and the consequent need to make every effort to avert the danger of such a war and to take measures to safeguard the security of peoples,

Believing that the proliferation of nuclear weapons would seriously enhance the danger of nuclear war,

In conformity with resolutions of the United Nations General Assembly calling for the conclusion of an agreement on the prevention of wider dissemination of nuclear weapons,

Undertaking to cooperate in facilitating the application of International Atomic Energy Agency safeguards on peaceful nuclear activities,

Expressing their support for research, development, and other efforts to further the application, within the framework of the International Atomic Energy Agency safeguards system, of the principle of safeguarding effectively the flow of source and special fissionable materials by use of instruments and other techniques at certain strategic points,

Affirming the principle that the benefits of peaceful applications of nuclear technology, including any technological by-products which may be derived by nuclear-weapon States from the development of nuclear explosive devices, should be available for peaceful purposes to all Parties to the Treaty, whether nuclear-weapon or non–nuclear-weapon States.

Convinced that, in furtherance of this principle, all Parties to the Treaty are entitled to participate in the fullest possible exchange of scientific information for, and to contribute alone or in cooperation with other States to, the further development of the applications of atomic energy for peaceful purposes,

Declaring their intention to achieve at the earliest possible date the cessation of the nuclear arms race and to undertake effective measures in the direction of nuclear disarmament,

Urging the cooperation of all States in the attainment of this objective,

Recalling the determination expressed by the Parties to the 1963 Treaty banning nuclear weapon tests in the atmosphere in outer space and under water in its Preamble to seek to achieve the discontinuance of all test explosions of nuclear weapons for all time and to continue negotiations to this end,

Desiring to further the easing of international tension and the strengthening of trust between States in order to facilitate the cessation of the manufacture of nuclear weapons, the liquidation of all their existing stockpiles, and the elimination from national arsenals of nuclear weapons and the means of their delivery pursuant to a treaty on general and complete disarmament under strict and effective international control,

Recalling that, in accordance with the Charter of the United Nations, States must refrain in their international relations from the threat or use of force against the territorial integrity or political independence of any State, or in any other manner inconsistent with the Purposes of the United Nations, and that the establishment and maintenance of international peace and security are to be promoted with the least diversion for armaments of the world's human and economic resources,

Have agreed as follows:

ARTICLE I

Each nuclear-weapon State Party to the Treaty undertakes not to transfer to any recipient whatsoever nuclear weapons or other nuclear explosive devices or control over such weapons or explosive devices directly, or indirectly; and not in any way to assist, encourage, or induce any non–nuclear-weapons State to manufacture or otherwise acquire nuclear weapons or other nuclear explosive devices, or control over such weapons or explosive devices.

ARTICLE II

Each non–nuclear-weapon State Party to the Treaty undertakes not to receive the transfer from any transferor whatsoever of nuclear weapons or other nuclear explosive devices or of control over such weapons or explosives devices directly, or indirectly; nor to manufacture or otherwise acquire nuclear weapons or other nuclear explosive devices; and not to seek or receive any assistance in the manufacture of nuclear weapons or other nuclear explosive devices.

ARTICLE III

1. Each non–nuclear-weapon State Party to the Treaty undertakes to accept safeguards, as set forth in an agreement to be negotiated and concluded with the International Atomic Energy Agency in accordance with the Statute of the International Atomic Energy Agency and the Agency's safeguards system for the exclusive purpose of verification of the fulfillment of its obligations assumed under this Treaty with a view to preventing diversions of nuclear energy from peaceful uses to nuclear weapons or other nuclear explosive devices. Procedures for the safeguards required by this article shall be followed with respect to source or special fissionable material whether it is being produced, processed or used in any principal nuclear facility or is outside any such facility. The safeguards required by this article shall be applied on all source or special fissionable material in all peaceful nuclear activities within the territory of such State, under its jurisdiction, or carried out under its control anywhere.

2. Each State Party to the Treaty undertakes not to provide: (a) source or special fissionable material, or (b) equipment or material especially designed or prepared for the processing, use or production of special fissionable material, to any non–nuclear-weapon State for peaceful purposes, unless the source or special fissionable material shall be subject to the safeguards required by this article.

3. The safeguards required by this article shall be implemented in a manner designed to comply with article IV of this Treaty, and to avoid hampering the economic or technological development of the Parties or international cooperation in the field of peaceful nuclear activities, including the international exchange of nuclear material and equipment for the processing, use or production of nuclear material for peaceful purposes in accordance with the provisions of this article and the principle of safeguarding set forth in the Preamble of the Treaty.

4. Non–nuclear-weapon States Party to the Treaty shall conclude agreements with the International Atomic Energy Agency to meet the requirements of this article either individually or together with other States in accordance with the Statute of the International Atomic Energy Agency. Negotiation of such agreements shall commence within 180 days from the original entry into force of this Treaty. For States depositing their instruments of ratification or accession after the 180–day period, negotiation of such agreements shall commence not later than the date of such deposit. Such agreements shall enter into force not later than eighteen months after the date of initiation of negotiations.

ARTICLE IV

1. Nothing in this Treaty shall be interpreted as affecting the inalienable right of all Parties to the Treaty to develop research, production, and

use of nuclear energy for peaceful purposes without discrimination and in conformity with articles I and II of this Treaty.

2. All the Parties to the Treaty undertake to facilitate, and have the right to participate in, the fullest possible exchange of equipment, materials, and scientific and technological information for the peaceful uses of nuclear energy. Parties to the Treaty in a position to do so shall also cooperate in contributing alone or together with other States Party to the Treaty, with due consideration for the needs of the developing areas of the world.

ARTICLE V

Each Party to the Treaty undertakes to take appropriate measures to ensure that, in accordance with this Treaty, under appropriate international observation and through appropriate international procedures, potential benefits from any peaceful applications of nuclear explosions will be made available to non–nuclear-weapon States Party to the Treaty on a non-discriminatory basis, and that the charge to such Parties for the explosive devices used will be as low as possible and exclude any charge for research and development. Non–nuclear-weapon States Party to the Treaty shall be able to obtain such benefits, pursuant to a special international agreement or agreements, through an appropriate international body with adequate representation of non–nuclear-weapon States. Negotiations on this subject shall commence as soon as possible after the Treaty enters into force. Non–nuclear-weapons States Party to the Treaty so desiring may also obtain such benefits pursuant to bilateral agreements.

ARTICLE VI

Each of the Parties to the Treaty undertakes to pursue negotiations in good faith on effective measures relating to the cessation of the nuclear arms race at an early date and to nuclear disarmament, and on a treaty on general and complete disarmament under strict and effective international control.

ARTICLE VII

Nothing in this Treaty affects the right of any group of States to conclude regional treaties in order to assure the total absence of nuclear weapons in their respective territories.

ARTICLE VIII

1. Any Party to the Treaty may propose amendments to this Treaty. The text of any proposed amendment shall be submitted to the Depositary Governments which shall circulate it to all Parties to the Treaty. Thereupon, if requested to do so by one or more of the Parties to the Treaty, the Depositary Governments shall convene a conference, to which they shall invite all the Parties to the Treaty, to consider such an amendment.

2. Any amendment to this Treaty must be approved by a majority of the votes of all the Parties to the Treaty, including the votes of all nuclear-weapon States Party to the Treaty and all other Parties which, on the date the amendment is circulated, are members of the Board of Governors of the International Atomic Energy Agency. The amendment shall enter into force for each Party that deposits its instrument of ratification of the amendment upon the deposit of such instruments of ratification of all nuclear-weapon States Party to the Treaty and all other Parties which, on the date the amendment is circulated, are members of the Board of Governors of the International Atomic Energy Agency. Thereafter, it shall enter into force for any Party upon the deposit of its instrument of ratification of the amendment.

3. Five years after the entry into force of this Treaty, a conference of Parties to the Treaty shall be held in Geneva, Switzerland, in order to review the operation of this Treaty with a view to assuring that the purposes of the Preamble and the provisions of the Treaty are being realized. At intervals of five years thereafter, a majority of the Parties to the Treaty may obtain, by submitting a proposal to this effect to the Depositary Governments, the convening of further conferences with the same objective of reviewing the operation of the Treaty.

ARTICLE IX

1. This Treaty shall be open to all States for signature. Any State which does not sign the Treaty before its entry into force in accordance with paragraph 3 of this article may accede to it at any time.

2. This Treaty shall be subject to ratification by signatory States. Instruments of ratification and instruments of accession shall be deposited with the governments of the United States of America, the United Kingdom of Great Britain and Northern Ireland and the Union of the Soviet Socialist Republics, which are hereby designated Depositary Governments.

3. This Treaty shall enter into force after its ratification by the States, the governments of which are designated Depositaries of the Treaty, and forty other States signatory to this Treaty and the deposit of their instruments of

ratification. For the purposes of this Treaty, a nuclear-weapon State is one which has manufactured and exploded a nuclear weapon or other nuclear explosive device prior to January 1, 1967.

4. For States whose instruments of ratification or accession are deposited subsequent to the entry into force of this Treaty, it shall enter into force on the date of the deposit of their instruments of ratification or accession.

5. The Depositary Governments shall promptly inform all signatory and acceding States of the date of each signature, the date of deposit of each instrument of ratification or of accession, the date of entry into force of this Treaty, and the date of receipt of any requests for convening a conference or other notices.

6. This Treaty shall be registered by the Depositary Governments pursuant to article 102 of the Charter of the United Nations.

ARTICLE X

1. Each Party shall in exercising its national sovereignty have the right to withdraw from the Treaty if it decides that extraordinary events, related to the subject matter of this Treaty, have jeopardized the supreme interests of its country. It shall give notice of such withdrawal to all other Parties to the Treaty and to the United Nations Security Council three months in advance. Such notice shall include a statement of the extraordinary events it regards as having jeopardized its supreme interests.

2. Twenty-five years after the entry into force of the Treaty, a conference shall be extended for an additional fixed period or periods. This decision shall be taken by a majority of the Parties to the Treaty.

ARTICLE XI

This Treaty, the English, Russian, French, Spanish, and Chinese texts of which are equally authentic, shall be deposited in the archives of the Depositary Governments. Duly certified copies of this Treaty shall be transmitted by the Depositary Governments to the Governments of the signatory and acceding States.

Further Reading

GENERAL WORKS ON NONPROLIFERATION

An excellent introduction to the nonproliferation field is found in William C. Potter, *Nuclear Power and Nonproliferation: An Interdisciplinary Perspective* (Cambridge, Mass.: Oelgeschlager, Gunn & Hain, Publishers, 1982). Despite its age, most of the technical, historical, political, economic, and strategic analysis in the volume are still valuable. Another useful volume from the same era is Lewis Dunn, *Controlling the Bomb: Nuclear Proliferation in the 1980's* (New Haven, Conn.: Yale University Press, 1982). A fine compilation of resources in the nonproliferation field is David H. Albright, comp., *The Nuts and Bolts of Nuclear Proliferation: A Guidebook* (New York: Center for War, Peace, and the News Media, 1991).

ON NUCLEAR PHYSICS, REACTORS, THE FUEL CYCLE, AND THE NUCLEAR BOMB

For a readable discussion of basic nuclear physics and the elements of nuclear weapons, see Thomas B. Cochran, William Arkin, and Milton Hoenig, *Nuclear Weapons Databook, Volume 1: U.S. Nuclear Forces and Capabilities* (Cambridge, Mass.: Ballinger Publishing Co., 1984). Historical accounts of the U.S. nuclear weapons program include Richard Rhodes, *The Making of the Atomic Bomb* (New York: Simon and Schuster, 1986) and Chuck Hansen, *US Nuclear Weapons: The Secret History* (New York: Orion Books, 1988). The nuclear fuel cycle is comprehensively described in Thomas B. Cochran, William Arkin, Robert S. Norris, and Milton Hoenig, *Nuclear Weapons Databook, Volume 2: U.S. Nuclear Warhead Production* (Cambridge, Mass.: Ballinger Publishing Co., 1984). For a readable description of basic nuclear reactor types, see Anthony Nero, *A Guidebook to Nuclear Reactors* (Berkeley: University of California Press,

1979). A lavishly illustrated description of nuclear physics, nuclear reactors, and the nuclear fuel cycle is found in Jacques Leclercq, with the assistance of Michel Durr, *The Nuclear Age* (Paris: Le Chene, 1986).

ON THE HISTORY OF NONPROLIFERATION

For a comprehensive account of postwar nonproliferation efforts, see McGeorge Bundy, *Danger and Survival* (New York: Random House, 1988). A French perspective on nuclear history is found in Bertrand Goldschmidt, *The Atomic Complex: A Worldwide Political History of Atomic Energy,* translated by Bruce M. Adkins (La Grange Park, Ill.: American Nuclear Society, 1982). A fine retrospective on the Atoms for Peace program is found in Joseph F. Pilat, Robert E. Pendley, and Charles K. Ebinger, eds., *Atoms for Peace: An Analysis After Thirty Years,* Westview Special Studies in International Relations (Boulder, Colo.: Westview Press, 1985). For the history of the IAEA and its role in the nonproliferation regime, see Lawrence Scheinman, *The International Atomic Energy Agency and World Nuclear Order* (Washington, D.C.: Resources for the Future, 1987). For a concise overview of the spread of nuclear weapons capabilities since World War II and the evolution of the nonproliferation regime, see Leonard Spector, *A Historical and Technical Introduction to the Proliferation of Nuclear Weapons* (Washington, D.C.: Carnegie Endowment for International Peace, 1992). More complete descriptions of the nuclear programs in nations of proliferation concern are found in Leonard S. Spector with Jacqueline R. Smith, *Nuclear Ambitions: The Spread of Nuclear Weapons 1989–1990* (Boulder, Colo.: Westview Press, 1990).

ON LEGAL STRUCTURES

An excellent analysis of major nonproliferation treaties is found in David A.V. Fischer, *The International Non-Proliferation Regime, 1987* (Geneva: United Nations Institute for Disarmament Research, 1987). Another excellent source, focusing solely on the NPT, is Jozef Goldblat, *Twenty Years of the Nonproliferation Treaty: Implementation and Prospects* (Oslo: International Peace Research Institute, 1990). For a comprehensive collection of nonproliferation documents, see Darryl Howlett and John Simpson, *Nuclear Non-Proliferation: A Reference Handbook* (Harlow: Longman Group UK Limited, 1992).

ON INTERNATIONAL SAFEGUARDS

The most comprehensive treatment of safeguards is found in David Fischer and Paul Szasz, *Safeguarding the Atom: A Critical Appraisal,* edited by

Jozef Goldblat (Stockholm: International Peace Research Institute, 1985). Shorter discussions of safeguards are found in David A.V. Fischer, *The International Non-Proliferation Regime, 1987* (Geneva: United Nations Institute for Disarmament Research, 1987); and Lawrence Scheinman, *The International Atomic Energy Agency and World Nuclear Order* (Washington, D.C.: Resources for the Future, 1987). The latter provides a fine discussion of the evolution of safeguards since the 1950s. The International Atomic Energy Agency publishes a series of pamphlets and booklets describing its safeguarding activities, one of which is Peter Kelly, *Safeguards in Europe* (Vienna: International Atomic Energy Agency, 1985).

ON THE POLITICS
OF NONPROLIFERATION

For a comprehensive analysis of the incentives and disincentives for pursuing a nuclear weapons capability, and of strategies for dealing with the proliferation, see William C. Potter, *Nuclear Power and Nonproliferation: An Interdisciplinary Perspective* (Cambridge, Mass.: Oelgeschlager, Gunn & Hain, Publishers, 1982); and Lewis Dunn, *Controlling the Bomb: Nuclear Proliferation in the 1980's* (New Haven, Conn.: Yale University Press, 1982). The "winning" nonproliferation strategy is articulated in Thomas W. Graham, "Winning the Nonproliferation Battle," *Arms Control Today* (September 1991), p. 8. For a review of the decisionmaking behind the nuclear programs of Sweden, South Korea, Japan, Israel, South Africa, and India, see Mitchell Reiss, *Without the Bomb: The Politics of Nuclear Nonproliferation* (New York: Columbia University Press, 1988). For an alternative view of proliferation, which regards the spread of nuclear weapons as a stabilizing phenomenon in international politics, see Kenneth N. Waltz, "The Spread of Nuclear Weapons: More May Be Better," *Adelphi Papers* (171: 1981).

ON THE NPT EXTENSION CONFERENCE

For a brief and excellent summary of the issues and alternatives facing delegates to the 1995 extension conference, see George Bunn, Charles Van Doren, and David Fischer, *Options and Opportunities: The NPT Extension Conference of 1995* (Southampton, UK: Programme for Promoting Nuclear Non-Proliferation, University of Southampton, 1991). The impact of a limited extension of the NPT in 1995 is described in John Simpson, ed., *Nuclear Non-Proliferation: An Agenda for the 1990s*, Ford/Southampton Studies in North/South Security Relations (Cambridge: Cambridge University Press, 1987).

ON NATIONS OF PROLIFERATION CONCERN

An excellent overview of the nuclear programs of selected nations of proliferation concern is found in Leonard Spector with Jacqueline Smith, *Nuclear Ambitions: The Spread of Nuclear Weapons, 1989–1990* (Boulder, Colo.: Westview Press, 1990). For a quarterly survey of nuclear-related trade developments in selected nations of proliferation concern, see *Eye on Supply,* published by the Emerging Nuclear Suppliers Project, Monterey Institute of International Studies, Monterey, Calif. A comprehensive quarterly survey of the proliferation developments around the world is given in *PPNN Newsbrief,* published by the Programme for Promoting Nuclear Non-Proliferation, University of Southampton, Southampton, UK. Developments in the former Soviet Union are documented in *Cooperative Denuclearization: From Pledges to Deeds* (Cambridge, Mass.: CSIA Studies in International Security No. 2, John F. Kennedy School of Government, Harvard University, 1993).

ON CURRENT CHALLENGES
TO THE NONPROLIFERATION REGIME

A weekly survey of nuclear-related developments, with an emphasis on the commercial nuclear industry, is found in *Nucleonics Week,* published by McGraw-Hill, Inc., New York. For a comprehensive quarterly survey of proliferation developments around the world, see *PPNN Newsbrief,* published by the Programme for Promoting Nuclear Non-Proliferation, University of Southampton, Southampton, UK. For a weekly translation of foreign media reports on proliferation developments, see *Proliferation Issues,* published by the Foreign Broadcast Information Service, Washington, D.C. An excellent survey of plutonium stocks around the world is found in David Albright, Frans Berkhout, and William Walker, *World Inventory of Plutonium and Highly Enriched Uranium, 1992* (Oxford: Oxford University Press, 1993).

Glossary

Atoms for Peace. The U.S.-sponsored nuclear program launched in 1953 to share nuclear materials and technology for peaceful purposes with other nations. The program was a turnabout from previous U.S. nuclear policy, which sought to prohibit the dissemination of nuclear-related knowledge and technology.

Baruch Plan. The U.S.-sponsored initiative to outlaw nuclear weapons and to internationalize global stocks of fissile material for use in peaceful nuclear programs. After it was proposed in 1946, the United States and former Soviet Union held negotiations on the program but never reached agreement. The initiative died in 1949.

Challenge inspections. A colloquial term used to designate unscheduled inspections of nuclear facilities carried out at the request of another nation. Known formally under the Treaty of Tlatelolco as "special inspections," these are different from the NPT's special inspections, which are not automatically carried out at the request of another state.

Conversion. A stage of the nuclear fuel cycle in which uranium is converted from its milled form, called "yellowcake," to uranium oxide or uranium metal (for use in a heavy-water reactor) or uranium hexafluoride (for enrichment and use in a light-water reactor).

Coolant. The material in the reactor core used to draw out heat to run a turbine and produce electricity.

Critical mass. In a nuclear explosive, the minimum amount of fissile material needed to sustain a chain reaction. Subcritical amounts of fissile material allow too many neutrons to escape the material before a chain reaction can be established.

Depleted uranium. Uranium with less U-235 than that found in uranium ore. In the enrichment process, U-235 atoms are extracted from one batch of gasified uranium and transferred to a different batch. The uranium with the increased proportion of U-235 is called "enriched," whereas the U-235-poor batch is "depleted."

Dual-use items. Items, materials, or technologies that can be used in nuclear as well as nonnuclear endeavors. Their possible use in nonnuclear endeavors makes these items difficult to regulate.

Enrichment (of uranium). The process whereby the percentage of U-235 atoms in uranium is increased from its natural level of 0.7 percent. The greater the percentage of fissile U-235 in uranium, the more likely the uranium can sustain a fission chain reaction.

Fertile material. Material that can become fissionable after absorbing a neutron. U-238, a fertile material, becomes fissionable Pu-239 after taking in an extra neutron.

Fissile material. Fissionable material the nuclei of which are able to be split by neutrons of various speeds. Uranium-233, Uranium-235, and Plutonium-239 are all fissile materials. Fissile materials fission more easily than other fissionable materials, and are more desirable for most reactor types and essential for nuclear explosives.

Fission. The splitting of an atom, which releases tremendous amounts of energy. Compare to fusion.

Fission bomb. A nuclear weapon that uses fission (as opposed to fusion) for the violent and uncontrolled release of tremendous amounts of energy.

Fissionable material. Nuclear material the nuclei of which are able to be split (fissionable) only by fast neutrons. Uranium-238 and Thorium-232 are both fissionable materials.

Fuel cycle. The various stages in the life of uranium or plutonium as they relate to the functioning of a nuclear reactor. These stages range from the mining of uranium ore to the disposal of nuclear waste.

Fuel fabrication. A stage of the nuclear fuel cycle in which uranium or plutonium is fashioned into fuel rods for use in a nuclear reactor.

Fuel rods. The metal tubes containing pellets of uranium or plutonium fuel that are burned in the reactor core.

Full-scope safeguards. Safeguards that apply to all the fissile material in a nation. Compare with item-only safeguards.

Fusion. The melding of two atoms, which produces extraordinary amounts of energy. Compare with fission.

Glenn Amendment. A section of the U.S. Congress International Security Assistance Act of 1977, which revised the Symington Amendment of 1976 to include a provision terminating U.S. assistance to any NPT non–nuclear weapon state that detonates a nuclear explosive.

Heavy water. Water whose atoms contain an extra neutron when compared to atoms of "light," or ordinary, water. Heavy water is an ideal moderator because its neutron-saturated atoms absorb few of the neutrons used to fission uranium atoms. This makes possible the use of natural uranium to run a heavy-water reactor.

Highly enriched uranium (HEU). Uranium whose percentage of U-235 has been raised from its natural level of 0.7 percent to 20 percent or higher.

Hot cells. Chambers designed for handling highly radioactive material using robotic arms, which are controlled from outside the cell. Hot cells are usually used in the processing of spent fuel.

Hydrogen bomb. A nuclear weapon that uses fusion, rather than fission, as the principal event to release an extraordinary amount of destructive energy. A hydrogen bomb is many times more destructive than a fission bomb.

INFCIRC/66. The model safeguards agreement used by the IAEA to safeguard individual nuclear facilities. It was most widely employed prior to the advent of nonproliferation treaties in the 1960s that required full-scope safeguards.

INFCIRC/153. The model safeguards agreement used by the IAEA for safeguards on all fissile material in a nation. It is the standard safeguards agreement associated with the NPT, the Treaty of Tlatelolco, and the Treaty of Rarotonga.

Isotopes. Molecules of the same family. U-233, U-235, and U-238 are all uranium isotopes.

Isotopic separation. The process of separating certain isotopes from others, as in uranium enrichment, in which some of the isotope U-238 is separated from U-235 in a batch of uranium.

Item-only safeguards. Safeguards that cover only a particular nuclear material or facility. Compare to full-scope safeguards.

Light water. Ordinary H_2O, used as a coolant and moderator in some types of reactors. Such reactors require enriched uranium fuel.

London Club. See Nuclear Suppliers Group.

Low-enriched uranium (LEU). Uranium with a U-235 content of less than 20 percent but greater than the natural level of 0.7 percent.

McMahon Act. The 1946 U.S. legislation that outlawed the transfer of nuclear materials, technologies, and know-how to other nations. It remained in effect until 1954.

Mixed-oxide (MOX) fuel. Nuclear fuel that contains a mixture of uranium and plutonium. The plutonium content in MOX fuel is of particular proliferation concern.

Moderator. The material in a nuclear reactor that surrounds the fuel and acts as a buffer to slow-flying neutrons. Once the neutrons have decelerated, they are able to imbed themselves in fissile atoms, destabilizing the atoms and causing them to split, or fission.

Natural uranium. Uranium of any type prior to enrichment. It includes uranium ore, yellowcake, uranium oxide, uranium metal, and unenriched uranium hexafluoride.

Non–nuclear weapon states (NNWS). A legal term used in the NPT to refer to nations that had not detonated a nuclear explosive prior to 1967.

NPT review conferences. Conferences held every five years since 1975 to assess the implementation of the Nuclear Non-Proliferation Treaty.

Nuclear Suppliers Group. A group of nuclear supplier nations that works to coordinate trade policies in order to ensure that nuclear materials and technologies are used for peaceful purposes.

Nuclear weapon–free zone. A geographical area in which nuclear weapons are not allowed to be built, possessed, transferred, or tested.

Nuclear weapon states (NWS). A legal term used in the NPT to refer to nations that had detonated a nuclear device prior to 1967. By this definition, only China, France, the former Soviet Union (now Russia), the United Kingdom, and the United States are NWS.

Peaceful nuclear explosion (PNE). Nuclear explosion carried out for non-military purposes, such as the construction of harbors or canals. Because PNEs are technically indistinguishable from nuclear explosions of a military nature, they are highly restricted in several nonproliferation treaties.

Plutonium-239. The plutonium isotope best suited for use in a nuclear bomb. Pu-239 is not found in nature; it is created when U-238 atoms in the reactor fuel absorb a neutron.

Plutonium-240. The plutonium isotope formed when Pu-239 absorbs a neutron rather than fissioning. It is less desirable than Pu-239 for use in a nuclear bomb.

Production reactor. A nuclear reactor whose primary purpose is the production of high-grade plutonium. Any reactor can produce plutonium for use in a nuclear weapon, but the plutonium emanating from a production reactor is ideal for making bombs. Also known as a "plutonium production reactor."

Pursuit. A legal concept denoting the legal "contagiousness" of safeguards, whereby safeguards tend to spread to unsafeguarded nuclear material. For example, nuclear material processed or derived from safeguarded material is then also subject to safeguards. In addition, safeguarded material introduced into an unsafeguarded nuclear plant "infects" the rest of the plant, bringing all material in the entire plant under safeguards.

Reprocessing (of plutonium). The procedure whereby plutonium is extracted from spent fuel. Sometimes more descriptively referred to as "plutonium extraction."

Research reactor. A small reactor, usually less than 10 MW, used for research purposes rather than power production.

Special inspections. Unscheduled nuclear inspections at sites originally agreed upon by the state and the inspection authority.

Spent fuel. Nuclear fuel taken from a reactor after burn-up. It is rich in plutonium and other radioactive elements.

Symington Amendment. A part of the U.S. Congress International Security and Arms Export Control Act of 1976, which requires termination of economic and military assistance to countries importing sensitive nuclear technologies without first accepting full-scope safeguards.

Thorium. A nuclear material that eventually becomes U-233, a fissionable material, after absorbing a neutron.

Tritium. A nuclear material that facilitates fissioning and increases the yield of a nuclear explosion. It is also used to reduce the quantity of fissionable material needed to create an atomic bomb.

Uranium-233. A fissionable uranium isotope not found in nature. It is formed when Thorium-232 absorbs a neutron, and is used as reactor fuel.

Uranium-235. A fissionable uranium isotope highly desirable for use in a nuclear reactor or nuclear bomb. U-235 constitutes only a tiny portion of the atoms in a chunk of natural uranium. For use in most reactors and nuclear weapons, U-235 must be gleaned from large batches of uranium in order to accumulate the quantities necessary to sustain a fission chain reaction.

Uranium-238. A fertile uranium isotope not usually prone to fissioning and not usable in a nuclear bomb. U-238 constitutes more than 99 percent of the isotopes in natural uranium.

Uranium hexafluoride (UF_6). Natural uranium and fluorine. When heated, UF_6 becomes a gas, which can be used to make enriched uranium.

Weapons-grade material. Uranium enriched to 93 percent U-235 and plutonium with a very high concentration of Pu-239. These materials give ideal performance (in terms of efficiency and yield) in a nuclear bomb.

Weapons-usable material. Uranium or plutonium that can be used in a nuclear bomb, whether or not it is weapons-grade. The plutonium extracted from the fuel rods of a typical light-water reactor, for example, contains impurities and a relatively low level of Pu-239, which make it weapons-usable but not weapons-grade. Also known as reactor-grade material.

Yellowcake. Processed but not enriched uranium. It is usable as nuclear fuel in reactors that run on unenriched uranium.

Zangger Committee. A committee of NPT nuclear supplier nations set up in 1971 to interpret Article III.2 of the NPT, which deals with safeguards requirements for treaty parties. The committee is an ad hoc group and its findings are not binding on treaty parties. However, its work is respected and its recommendations accepted by most NPT nuclear supplier states.

Zirconium. A metal used to make fuel rod casings.

Index

About the Book and the Author

This accessible overview of the technical and political dimensions of nuclear nonproliferation is particularly significant in light of such urgent challenges to the nonproliferation regime as North Korea's withdrawal from the Nuclear Non-Proliferation Treaty (NPT), Iraq's tenacity in pursuit of nuclear weapons, and Ukraine's reluctance to part with its inherited nuclear arsenal.

Gardner guides the student of arms control painlessly through the fundamentals of nuclear physics, nuclear reactors, and the nuclear fuel cycle in language familiar to any interested reader. He likewise explains clearly the evolution of the nuclear nonproliferation regime, the system of international nuclear safeguards, and the prospects for the extension of the NPT in 1995.

The *Primer* includes information on the status of nuclear programs in the nations of greatest proliferation concern, a glossary, and the full text of the NPT.

Gary T. Gardner is a consultant to the World Bank. Previously, he managed the Soviet Nonproliferation Project and was research assistant on the Emerging Nuclear Suppliers Project at the Monterey Institute of International Studies.

*Other Publications of the MIIS Program
for Nonproliferation Studies*

Edward Laurance. *The International Arms Trade.* Lexington Books, 1992.

William C. Potter. *Nuclear Profiles of the Soviet Successor States.* Monterey Institute of International Studies, 1993.

William C. Potter and Harlan Jencks, eds. *The International Missile Bazaar: The New Suppliers' Network.* Westview Press, 1993.